P9-EDX-884

More Colonial Women

ALSO BY CAROLE CHANDLER WALDRUP
AND FROM MCFARLAND

*Colonial Women: 23 Europeans
Who Helped Build a Nation* (1999)

*The Vice Presidents: Biographies of the 45 Men
Who Have Held the Second Highest
Office in the United States* (1996)

*Presidents' Wives: The Lives of 44
American Women of Strength* (1989)

More Colonial Women

25 Pioneers of Early America

CAROLE CHANDLER WALDRUP

McFarland & Company, Inc., Publishers
Jefferson, North Carolina, and London

LIBRARY OF CONGRESS CATALOGUING-IN-PUBLICATION DATA

Waldrup, Carole Chandler, 1925–
   More Colonial women : 25 pioneers of early America /
Carole Chandler Waldrup.
      p.   cm.
   Includes bibliographical references and index.

   ISBN 0-7864-1839-7 (softcover : 50# alkaline paper)

   1. United States—History—Colonial period, ca. 1600–1775—
Biography. 2. Women—United States—Biography. I. Title.
E187.5.W36   2004
920.72'0973'09032—dc22   2004009828

British Library cataloguing data are available

©2004 Carole Chandler Waldrup. All rights reserved

*No part of this book may be reproduced or transmitted in any form
or by any means, electronic or mechanical, including photocopying
or recording, or by any information storage and retrieval system,
without permission in writing from the publisher.*

Cover image: ©2004 clipart.com

Manufactured in the United States of America

McFarland & Company, Inc., Publishers
  Box 611, Jefferson, North Carolina 28640
   www.mcfarlandpub.com

CONTENTS

Contents

PREFACE

I enjoyed writing this book because the lives of the various women were so different from the one I know. It is difficult in many cases to understand how these women even survived, given all the hardships they faced. I think it is helpful to remind people how much easier life today is.

In her own way, each woman profiled here contributed to the development of our country. Most of the men they lived and worked alongside—among them Ben Franklin, Andrew Jackson, Daniel Boone, and William Penn—have been honored over and over, while their own names, almost without exception, are unknown to most citizens of the United States.

In this book and in the one that preceded it, *Colonial Women: 23 Europeans Who Helped Build a Nation,* I have made a small effort to change that.

1

LUCY WINTHROP DOWNING
(1600–1679)

Lucy Winthrop was a sister of John Winthrop, one of the founders of the Massachusetts Bay colony. She was born on January 9, 1600, at Groton Manor in the Suffolk district of England. Her father was Adam Winthrop and her mother was the former Anne Browne.

Lucy stayed in England for eight years after her brother came to the New World in 1630. She married Emanuel Downing on April 10, 1622, in Groton. Emanuel had been married before and had three children with that wife; they were John, Susan and Mary.

As time passed, Lucy and Emanuel had children also—nine in all. They had a son named George born in 1623, a daughter Lucy born in 1625, twins Joshua and Nicholas, born in 1627, Robert born in 1628, Adam and Henry, also twins, born in 1630, daughter Anne born in 1633 and Martha in 1636.

Emanuel Downing was working as a lawyer in Dublin, Ireland, when John Winthrop left England in 1630. Emanuel was an attorney of the Inner Temple in London, having graduated from the law school at Cambridge University.

Lucy had no great desire to bring her family to join her brother and his family in Massachusetts, but John kept pressuring Emanuel to emigrate.

Lucy wrote Margaret, John's wife, in 1636: "I harty-lie thank you for all the expressions of your love and desires of our company. I know not yet how it will please God to dispose of us ... my present condition is unfit for changes...."

To her brother John she wrote: "but I must deal plainlie with you, and let you know that many good people here, and some that understand New England reasonable well, both by sight and relations of friends, that are able to judg, they do much fear the country cannot afford subsistence for many people, and that if you were not supplyed of incomes from hence, your lives would be very miserable...."

Near the end of 1636, as Governor Winthrop apparently increased the pressure to join him and his family in New England, Lucy wrote: "George [her son] and his father complye more cordially for New England; but, poor boy, I fear that journey would not be so prosperous for him as I could wish in respect that you have no societies ... for the education of youths in learning; and I bless God for it, he is yet reasonable hopeful in that way. ... [I]t would make me go far nimbler to New England if God should call me to it than otherwise I should, and I believ a colledge would put no small life into the plantation."

Lucy's letter must have had some influence, for on October 28th of that same year, the General Court of Massachusetts agreed to allot 400 pounds to establish a "schoole or colledge" in Newtown nearby. Newtown would also be the name of the school.

Two years later, in 1638, the name was changed to Cambridge, and soon after that they decided the college "shall be called Harvard College."

In November of 1638 Lucy and Emanuel arrived, with their children, in Salem, Massachusetts, on the *Thomas and Francis*. Emanuel lost no time in buying 300 acres of land in the Peabody area of the Salem colony, and he had a house built on it for his family. They called the estate "Groton," after Lucy's old home in England

Young George Downing enrolled in Harvard College, and graduated in 1642. He was second in his class of nine in academic standing. He returned to England three years later and became a spy for Lord Oliver Cromwell, who would later be named Lord Protector of England.

When King Charles I of England was executed by his enemies in 1649, during the English Civil War, Cromwell hoped to establish a new dynasty. He succeeded, but after Cromwell died in 1658, his son, Richard Cromwell, resigned as his father's successor. As a result, King Charles II came to the English throne in 1660.

Meanwhile, in the Massachusetts colony, Lucy Downing and Margaret Winthrop continued their correspondence between visits. Lucy wrote Margaret to thank her for gifts of rosemary and apples, and added, "Your lemmons were allmost as rare as drops of life. I am all the more sensible of your deprivement of them."

The Downings' home in Peabody was destroyed by fire in 1645, along with a large store of the colony's gunpowder on the property. As soon as possible, Emanuel rebuilt their home for his family, as well as houses for workmen and tenants. Since coming to Massachusetts, Lucy had given birth to three more children, John and Dorcas (1640), and Theophilus (1644).

Lucy's letters showed her sense of humor at times, as when she said she would prefer her next child to be born an "Indyan than a London Coknye."

Emanuel was allowed to distill "strong water" in 1648, and he used a house nearby on old Ipswich Road for a tavern.

Lucy wrote,

> Our stilling I think might be pritty strong, but that all the rye
> was eaten up almost before the Indian (corn) was gathered.
> Could you teach us how to kern (grind) rye out of the seawater?
> That I question not would make the still vapor (go) as far as
> Pecoite (Pequot), and the Indians I believ would like that smoak
> very well, for the English have but two objections against it.
> One—it's too dear (costly) and two—there's not enough of it.
> Cure these and we might all have employment enough at
> Salem, and as it is we could have custom ten times more than
> pay.

Lucy was a tidy, industrious woman and a good housewife, but she criticized her step-daughter Mary's ineptitude in caring for

Mary's brother's laundry. Fortunately, before conditions became too unpleasant, Mary married Anthony Stoddard; he was considered to be a very good choice.

When John Winthrop, Jr., came back to New England, Emanuel invested in his ironworks, lead mines and saltworks.

From 1646 to 1656, Emanuel and Lucy lived with their children in a house in Salem. Later Governor Simon Bradstreet and his family lived there from 1676 to 1697.

Emanuel went back to England in 1656, leasing his farm and tavern to John Proctor. He had owned the property since his arrival in 1638.

After Emanuel had made his ninth voyage back to England in 1656, he received an appointment as Clerk of Council of State in Scotland. He and Lucy remained in Edinburgh, until he died on September 26, 1660, at age 75. He was returned to London for burial.

Several months after his death, Lucy also returned to England to live, and her son George provided her a home in East Hatley. She died on April 10, 1679, at age 79 and was buried in England.

Bibliography

Earle, Alice Morse. *Margaret Winthrop.* Williamston, Mass.: Corner House, 1975.

Web Site: www. downingfamily.org Emanuel1%20Downing.htm

2

ELIZABETH READE WINTHROP
(1614–1672)

Elizabeth Reade was young John Winthrop, Jr.'s second wife. His first wife, Martha Fones, died within four years of their wedding while giving birth to their daughter, who also died. John and Martha were living in Massachusetts at the time, having left England in 1631.

John was sincerely and deeply grieved by Martha's death and spent a period during which he attended no public meetings and withdrew from daily duties. When the Massachusetts Bay colony needed someone to represent them in a Parliamentary charter hearing in England in October 1634, young John was asked to go, along with the Reverend John Wilson. The Winthrop family was glad to get the young man away from the scene of his tragedy for a while.

John was supposed to make sure the English government did not revoke the charter for the Massachusetts colony. He was told to assure officials that the territory was being adequately defended against other nations and that all citizens were loyal to the Crown.

After reaching England, young John also occupied his time with business matters for his stepmother, Margaret, and acted as agent in disposing of property belonging to Captain John Endicott, then living in Salem in the Massachusetts colony.

It was during these negotiations that John met pretty Elizabeth Reade. Her stepfather, Hugh Peter, was the best known nonconformist religious believer in England, and was a supporter of the efforts to reform religion in New England. He advised young Winthrop on steps to take to quiet questions from English authorities about religious activities in the Massachusetts Bay area.

John met with Hugh Peter at his home and elsewhere, and as the weeks passed, he and Elizabeth fell in love. Elizabeth married John on July 6, 1635, in the Church of St. Matthew in London, after all the necessary investigations into prospects and social status had been completed.

Elizabeth Reade had been born in November 1614, in Wickford in Essex, to Edmund and Elizabeth Cooke Reade. Elizabeth was probably taught basic educational subjects by a tutor, but she was only able to write a little, and that with difficulty. (Surviving examples of her writing, however, were written when she was in her fifties, and she could have suffered from arthritis or some other crippling disease in her hands.)

Elizabeth was better suited for colonial adventures than Martha, her predecessor, had been. Elizabeth was calm, well-mannered and an excellent housekeeper. She was well-versed in the Scriptures and a devout Puritan. She was also a sturdier, healthier woman than Martha, who had benign delicate health and reportedly cried often.

While he was negotiating as an agent of the Massachusetts Bay colony, young John received an unexpected offer. A group of English investors asked him to undertake the establishment of a new colony and trading post on the Connecticut River, and to be governor. After serious thought, he accepted the offer.

In October 1635, young John and his new bride reached the New World on the ship Abigail. John must have had some second thoughts about the reactions of his father and other Massachusetts officials to the news he was bringing them. The good news was that their charter was safe for the time being, but the bad news was that he would be launching a new colony and trading post nearby, in competition with theirs!

The newlyweds stayed in Boston when they first arrived and John, Jr., did not start on his projected colony in Connecticut until the latter part of March 1636. Elizabeth was now pregnant with their first child, so he went exploring into the new territory with a party of men, and left her in Boston with family members to take care of her.

Having heard earlier that Dutch explorers were moving into the lower Connecticut River region, John had sent an advance group to establish ownership in November 1635. The group openly unloaded a stock of ammunition and staked a claim to the area. The 2000 pounds John had brought back, which had been furnished by his English backers, went a long way in obtaining men and action at the right time.

The first colony in Connecticut was at Saybrook. All was not perfect, however, as the workmen complained about their living quarters, the monotony of their diet and the lack of sufficient clothes to keep them warm. The complaint that he had failed to furnish a place for worship headed the list of their grievances. Governor John Winthrop in Boston must have been shocked that his own son would fall short in any area of religion.

When Elizabeth gave birth to their first child, a daughter they named Elizabeth but called Betty, John left Saybrook in the hands of workmen and returned to Boston. As soon as his wife was able to travel, they went to live in his former home in Ipswich, while the Saybrook colony slowly took shape at the hands of his workmen.

In March 1638, their son Fitz-John was born in Ipswich and another daughter they named Lucy was born in 1639.

Elizabeth was not much more content living at Ipswich than Martha had been. It seemed the wind blew endlessly over the marshes, and the cold penetrated the many cracks in the walls of their crude house. Elizabeth took every opportunity she could to return to Boston to visit the elder Winthrops in their warmer house.

Young John found he enjoyed having his store of books at hand in Ipswich, but the recurring religious controversies there bored him.

He felt more discomfort and distaste for the religious problems in Boston that led to the banishment of Anne Hutchinson from the town in 1637. Even though he was fined, young John failed to attend any public assemblies for the next year. Despite his truancy, he was re-elected as a member of the Assembly in the summer of 1638, and in the fall he began attending again.

While his father seemed obsessed by religious matters and punishing sinners, young John was repelled by the fervor of his father. Instead, he turned his attention to scientific pursuits. He started a salt plant near Salem not long after he and Elizabeth arrived in Massachusetts.

Later he went back to England and sold some land he had there to obtain money to open an ironworks in Massachusetts. His second son, Wait-Still, was born in 1642 while he was away on business. Elizabeth wrote him that she managed to "beare his absence very well before company," but she added she cried often and yearned for him to come home.

Surprisingly, young John continued to be re-elected as one of the many assistant governors of the Massachusetts Bay government, even though he was away for months at a time.

When he returned the next year, he bought property at Ten Hills near the Mystic River and nearer his father's home. In September 1644, Mary Winthrop was born there.

Elizabeth's older sister, Margaret Lake, joined the household the next year. She and her husband, John Lake, had been living in Saybrook, but they had recently separated.

For all his talents and unquestioned abilities, young John could not seem to settle down to one location or occupation for long. He was restless by nature.

In October 1646, he moved his family yet again—this time to Fisher's Island near the mouth of the Connecticut River. The next month a major hurricane wreaked havoc in their region and other parts of New England.

They lived in the house there for the next several years, during which time their daughter Mary died at the age of eight. Elizabeth never liked the house after that, and she made no protest when her husband mentioned moving again.

The family moved to New Haven and a much better house about 1656. Young John established an ironworks there, and he and Elizabeth believed they had found a permanent home.

Friends in New London begged them to return there to live and offered to "sett up a Forge here, which may be one means to bring you backe again". They urged Elizabeth to use her wifely influence to get John to come back.

The elder John Winthrop died in 1649. On May 21, 1657, the officials in Hartford asked John, Jr., to be governor of all of the Connecticut colony. He was sorely tempted to accept. New Haven's religious practices were burdensome to him with the insistence that all citizens had to worship for hours on the Sabbath, during which day all travel and any labor were strictly forbidden, including bed making, cooking and even shaving.

On the other hand, Elizabeth was happier in New Haven than she had been anywhere else. John accepted the post as governor later in 1657, and when they sold their New Haven home two years later, Elizabeth was frank in saying she was sorry "that they could not accommodate matters so that we might live in New Haven," in a letter she wrote to her son Wait-Still, now a student at Harvard.

John continued to have interests other than colonial politics and religion. He was a student of astronomy, alchemy and mining for precious metals and minerals. He founded an ironworks at Lynn that he called Hammersmith. Soon the plant was producing enough iron to supply the Connecticut colony.

Fitz-John Winthrop was denied admission to Harvard due to academic deficiency. His father hired Thomas Dudley, Jr., to tutor Fitz, but he never became an intellectual.

However, Fitz was not as much worry to his parents as was their daughter Betty. She had been courting for most of 1657 and into 1658 a young clergyman named Antipas Newman. The Reverend Mr. Newman had been called recently to be the pastor of a church in Wenham, Massachusetts, and he wanted Betty to go with him as his wife.

Elizabeth was on the side of Betty and the course of true love, but John was only cautiously agreeable. Fitz and Wait were violently opposed to the match. Wait wrote Fitz in September 1659, that he thought Newman was "far inferiorre" to Betty.

Despite their objections, Betty's parents were more practical. Her father made arrangements to deed some land he owned near Salem to the couple as a dowry, and Elizabeth and her sister helped Betty collect some household necessities.

11

Betty married Antipas Newman in Wenham on November 11, 1658. Neither of her parents attended, as marriages were considered to be only civil affairs at that time and were not festive family events.

Betty and her new husband settled into married life happily and had a contented life together. Eventually they became the parents of six children, only one of whom died in infancy. However, that child, a daughter, was their first—and Elizabeth's first grandchild. Elizabeth became ill for a time from her deep grief.

When young Lucy Winthrop married Edward Palmes, a merchant in New London, both John and Elizabeth approved.

In 1672, Margaret Lake died from some variety of influenza. She was still living with Elizabeth and John at the time. Betty's husband, Antipas, also died in October of that same year, and on December 1, 1672, Elizabeth Winthrop died at age 58 in the new home they had recently built in New London.

John was crushed by Elizabeth's death. They had been married for more than 37 years and had reared a family together. He wrote to his recently widowed daughter, Betty: "Thus God is pleased to deprive us of our best earthly enjoyments that we might seriously seek for our chief support in Him and be weaned more from this world and these fading things below. My loss is irreparable."

During the war with King Phillip and his tribe of Narragansetts in 1675-76, Edward Palmes was in command of a company of militia comprising 2000 men, and Fitz Winthrop was put in command of all the soldiers of New London County by his father, who was still the governor of Connecticut. Wait was in charge of a company also, which included some Indians from another tribe.

King Philip's war was bloody and awful, and some 9000 people died, two-thirds of them Indians. Twelve colonial towns were completely destroyed, and a number of Indian villages were wiped out.

Such massive carnage saddened John. After living in peace for almost 50 years, all the elements of friendship between New England settlers and their Indian neighbors had been destroyed.

John Winthrop, Jr., died on April 5, 1676. He had been in failing health for some time, but had continued to be active until his death at age 70.

Bibliography

Black, Robert C. *The Younger John Winthrop*. New York: Columbia University Press, 1968.

Earle, Alice Morse. *Colonial Dames and Good Wives*. New York: Frederick Unger, 1962.

3

JUDITH GITON MANIGAULT
(1665–1711)

In 1670 the first group of people who were hoping to settle a colony in South Carolina arrived in the area, led by Joseph West. The first colonists were from England, but they had come to the New World by way of Barbados. The next year, Barbados natives also joined the colony, which later developed into the city of Charleston. This trend would continue for many years.

Joseph West was the colony's first governor, and he was an excellent leader. He helped arrange trade with nearby Indians, who furnished a steady supply of furs to sell for income. He encouraged experimentation with various crops for the area to find those most suitable. The best crops proved to be corn and other grains and vegetables. Livestock flourished and so did shipbuilding, with a plentiful supply of wood on hand in the nearby forests.

In 1685 rice seed was brought from Madagascar, and the crop grew magnificently in the fertile black swampland soil near the colony.

Food was available from colonists in other areas, as well as from the Indians, but it was very expensive. Housewives raised most of their own food, kept pigs for meat and cows for milk and butter as well as meat, and made their own butter and cheese.

Their love of beauty was shown in their flower beds, in which they grew lilies, carnations, tulips and roses.

Although English people were the first arrivals in South Carolina, in the late 1600s Scottish people and French Huguenots also came to live in the region. One of these immigrants of French Huguenot background was Judith Manigault.

Judith was born Judith Giton in La Voulte, the Languedoc, to French Huguenot parents about 1665. In October 1685, King Louis XIV of France decided to try to force the members of the Protestant sect to conform to Catholicism, the state religion of France.

Their resistance to the idea led to the repeal of the Edict of Nantes, which had guaranteed freedom of worship to the Huguenots. The king's actions caused thousands of these talented, energetic and industrious people to leave France forever.

Judith, her mother and her elder brother barely escaped ahead of a house-to-house search by government officials late in 1684. The oppressive atmosphere in France was such that they fled, leaving all their possessions except their clothing behind.

After a grueling nine-month sea voyage, Judith and her relatives reached Charleston in the South Carolina colony, and prepared to make their home there.

In 1685, not long after their arrival, Judith married Noe Royer, a weaver by trade, who was also a French Huguenot.

The young couple went to work clearing land for a homestead. Clearing land involved cutting down trees with axes or sawing them down, stripping off limbs and bark, digging up the stumps of the trees still in the ground and building some sort of shelter as they worked.

It was difficult, punishing work, and Judith became extremely discouraged. She wrote to another of her brothers who had emigrated to Holland: "Everything went wrong. Our elder brother died of the fever. We bore every kind of affliction, illness and plague, hunger, poverty and hard work. I have had no bread to eat for six months and have tilled the soil like a slave...."

Life was difficult for all the settlers in the southern colonies, despite the warmer climate and better farming conditions, because of the variety of feverish illnesses endemic to the area, many of which were transmitted by mosquitoes, considered by many to also be a plague.

Noe Royer died after he and Judith had been married for only three years. They had no children.

In 1699 Judith married another French Huguenot named Pierre Manigault. Pierre had managed to bring some money with him when he left France, and he bought a house for their home. A little later, he began a distillery business and then a cooperage to make the barrels he needed for his beverages.

Judith turned their home into an inn or boarding house for travelers coming to the area, and she even kept some children. The operation of an inn required the same talents as keeping a regular family home, but on a larger scale. It was a logical occupation for a woman.

The inns were important to the community because travelers brought news from the outside world, businessmen held meetings there, and often the social life of a colony centered around an inn.

Judith and Pierre had a son, born in 1704, whom they named Gabriel. It appeared life would be better here than what they had known before. They worked hard and the days were full, but they did not need to fear religious persecution and were free to worship with their fellow Huguenots.

It was the French colonists who brought artistic touches to home decorating in the New World. They were the first to cut worn-out clothing into strips and braid them into carpets. They made white and pastel-colored home fashions, as well as garments, and used mirrors as home accessories.

They tried valiantly to bring the industries of winemaking and silk manufacture to the New World, but were unsuccessful except on a very small scale. Many became teachers of dancing, art, manners and other social graces.

Art schools and needlework training were established, and they were soon followed by elementary schools, which covered basic educational subjects.

The Huguenots viewed life with good humor, and faced their onerous tasks in the colonies cheerfully. They stood in sharp contrast to the Puritans, who wore stern looks most of the time; but both would be vital developers of a new nation.

Judith may have been weakened by her earlier hardships, for she died in 1711 when her son was only seven years old.

Pierre was remarried in 1713 to Anne Reason, an English-woman, and they had a daughter they named Judith.

Pierre continued to prosper and soon built a second distillery. Later he built massive warehouses in the harbor area of Charleston and retail stores on the main street.

Gabriel inherited a substantial fortune when his father died in 1739, and he continued to operate the family businesses. He was said to be the richest man in South Carolina in the 1700s.

In time, Gabriel married and had a son named Peter, who went to Europe to be educated. While he was there, Eliza Pinckney and her husband, also from South Carolina, visited with young Peter. She wrote his mother about her son: "his polite and obliging behavior which we have experienced entitles him to all the returns his friends can make.... I dare assert, not only from mine, but from better judgments, he will make amends for all her cares and answer all her hopes."

Peter became Speaker of the House of Commons in South Carolina after his return home from England.

Sadly, Peter was killed in 1773 at age 42 while serving in the Continental Army. His estate inventory listed ownership of several plantations for a net worth of almost two million dollars (by 1977 calculations). He was a prominent South Carolina citizen who served as a member of the Assembly, Commissioner of Indian Affairs and as president of the Charles Town Library Society. He was also a generous contributor to St. Philip's Church, where he and his family worshipped.

When Charleston came under siege by British forces, Gabriel, along with Peter's young son, now 15 years old, offered to serve with the defenders of the city. Gabriel was then 75 years old.

Judith would have been proud of the men in her family if she could have foreseen the future. She was there to aid and guide them when they needed her, and she helped in their successes.

More Colonial Women

Bibliography

Hirsch, Arthur Henry, Ph.D. *The Huguenots of South Carolina.* Durham, N.C.: Duke University Press, 1928.
Weir, Robert M. *Colonial South Carolina, a History.* Millwood, N.Y.: KTO Press, 1983.

4

LYDIA LEE MATHER
(1670–1734)

Lydia Mather has been described as "mad" by historians for almost 300 years, a claim based entirely on her husband's diary entries. Lydia's second husband was Cotton Mather, a Puritan minister who viewed himself as correct in all respects; when anyone argued with him, he concluded that the person must be deranged.

Lydia Lee was born about 1670 in England, one of four daughters of Doctor Samuel Lee and his wife.

Doctor Lee and his family came to live in Bristol, in the Rhode Island colony, when he was invited to be minister of a church there in 1686.

Thanks to a large inheritance from his father, Doctor Lee did not have the financial struggles of many ministers, but was able to build a fine large home for his family. However, he must have been unhappy in the colonies, for he and his wife returned to England in 1689.

Within a few months of her arrival in Rhode Island, young Lydia Lee had married John George of Boston in 1687. Mr. George was a town selectman, merchant and exporter, and was able to support his new wife in a lavish style.

Lydia and John had one daughter, Katherine, who was born in 1692. About 1711 Katherine George married Nathan Howell, her father's business partner. In time they had two sons.

Lydia's husband John died in 1714 at age 49. He left Lydia the only beneficiary and executrix of his will, and Lydia was now a wealthy woman: John's partnership with Nathan Howell had been highly profitable.

Seven months later, on July 5, 1715, Lydia George married the Reverend Cotton Mather. It was a step down for her materially speaking, as she had been accustomed to a more luxurious way of life than she would have as a minister's wife. Lydia was Mather's third wife.

Lydia was more astute in business affairs than Cotton realized. She had a prenuptial contract drawn up which said that

> from and after the Consummation of the said Marriage, she, the said Lydia by herself, or with the assistance of such meet person or persons whom She shall appoint, shall and may from time to time and at all times during her Coverture, manage, impower and employ as she shall think fit, all the Lands, Tenements, money goods, Chattels or other Estate whatsoever which of right is belonging, appertaining or payable unto her, and to take, Receive and dispose to her own use all the Issues, profits, benefits and Incomes thence to be made or Raised without any Lett hindrance or denyall of the said Cotton Mather.

About three months after Lydia and Cotton were married, her daughter's husband, Nathan Howell, died. At age 23, Katherine Howell was left a widow with two sons to rear. She came to live with her mother and stepfather.

There were nine people living in the Mather household after the arrival of Katherine and her sons, including Abigail Mather, age 21, Hannah Mather, age 18, Elizabeth Mather, age 11, and Samuel Mather, age 9, as well as Lydia and Cotton. Lydia had not been accustomed to living with so many other people, but apparently she adjusted well to the confusion.

Cotton's marriage to Lydia was a real love match, at least on his part. He wrote in his diary that Lydia was "one that shines forever with a thousand Lovelinesses."

Their marriage began well enough. Cotton prayed with Lydia several times daily, he talked with her about the Scriptures, and he wrote in April 1716, "how happy am I in the conversation of so fine a Soul, and one so capable of soaring to the higher Flights of piety...."

Then Cotton was appointed to be the administrator of Nathan Howell's estate, at the request of Katherine Howell. That proved to be an unwise move on the part of everyone concerned, for Cotton Mather could not manage financial affairs well.

He strove earnestly to be a complete man of God; he was a highly successful minister in his church; but with his certainty that he was always right, he would have been difficult for any wife to live with.

Lydia managed to endure his extreme piety, but when she learned within some months that Cotton had apparently spent some of her daughter's money from Nathan Howell's estate, love flew out the window, at least temporarily.

Cotton had attended Harvard College in his youth, but he believed the school was now involved in teaching inappropriate subjects, such as Ethics, which Cotton characterized as "a vile piece of paganism."

Another school had been established at New Haven, and Cotton was interested in seeing the new college prosper.

On January 2, 1718, he wrote, "What shall I do ... for the welfare of the Colledge at New Haven? I am inclined to write to a wealthy East India merchant in London who may be disposed on several accounts to do for that Society and Colony."

The college at New Haven was becoming a favorite with most Puritans because of its strict observance of Calvinist doctrine.

Cotton wrote Elihu Yale in London on January 18 of that year: "certainly if what is forming at New Haven might wear the name of *Yale College*, it would be better than a name of someone's sons or daughters."

Elihu Yale considered the matter and decided that Cotton was right. It would be wonderful to have a college named in his honor, and Yale made a generous contribution to the school. Elihu's gift insured the survival and success of Yale College, now Yale University. The trustees did indeed name the college for its benefactor.

With so much enthusiasm for the new college, would Cotton have borrowed money from his stepdaughter's inheritance to make a sizable contribution of his own to Yale College? If he had done so, he would have been convinced he was following the will of God.

Cotton had written in his diary in November of that year that he planned to ask Lydia "what special Service for God and His Kingdome she will do, in case the Administration be well finished, and she find any Estate remaining, that may render her Capable of doing anything."

An entry in his journal in 1719 reads:

> The Consort, in whom I flattered myself with the View and Hopes of an uncommon Enjoyment, has dismally confirmed it unto me that our *Idols* must prove our *Sorrows*.
>
> Now and then, in some of the former Years, I observed and suffered grievous Outbreakings of her proud Passions, but I quickly overcame them, with my victorious Love, and in the Methods of Meekness and Goodness ... I do not know, that I have to this Day spoke one impatient or unbecoming Word unto her; tho' my Provocations have been unspeakable; and, it may be, few Men in the World, would have born them as I have done.
>
> But this last Year has been full of her prodigious paroxysms; which have made it a Year of such Distresses with me, and I have never seen in my life before....

Certainly something of a serious nature occurred, for Cotton wrote on November 21, 1718: "what I have hereto Relate is: That she had expressed such a venom against my Reserved Memorials, of experiences in, and projections for the Kingdom of God, as has obliged me to Lay the Memorials of this year, I thought, where she would not find them."

He goes on to accuse Lydia of stealing his journals and of making ink blots in others, most notably the entry in which he said he would ask how she would use the remainder of any of her inheritance.

We have only Cotton's word for what happened. He was fond of using the word "paroxysms" to describe the behavior of anyone who disagreed with him, as when Robert Calef criticized Cotton for trying to cure a young woman of demonic possession. Cotton said Calef caused "Paroxysms in the town." Similarly, when he met opposition for his stand on the reinstatement of the charter for Massachusetts, Cotton wrote that his opponents had "feverish paroxysms."

An accounting of the administration of the Howell estate was due on June 4, 1717, but there is no record of such an accounting until 1720.

On April 13, 1720, Judge Samuel Sewall received an anonymous letter, which was thought to have been sent by Cotton himself, which said:

> Your Honour I believe is not acquainted with his (Cotton's) troubles, but I find that which most overwhelms him is, ye wretched administration, as he calls it, in which he has been ensnared, by his Love to some whom he finds full of ingratitude.... But until your Honor shall release him, his condition, as he says, and I partly know it, is intolerable; every one yet knocks at his door surprises him, that his heart dies within him as he says, fearing there is an Arrest to be serv'd on him, or some body to dun him for a Debt, due from an Estate, which he nor his can be farther the better for ... he seems to be apprehensive of a strong plot laid to ruin him, by them for whom he always had yet bowels of a Tender father. He is commonly informed that your Nephew stirs up people to arrest him and has given ye Doctor reason to think, that he has consulted with an able Lawyer, to molest him for maladministration.... His Terrible wife (whose character Mr. Jon Sewall has given ... to others, and can give to your Honor if he pleases, will have a great Estate whether there be one or no.

The nephew to whom Cotton referred was Katherine Howell's new husband, also named Sewall.

In December 1720, Cotton had the prenuptial agreement that he had signed, notarized, confirming its denial to him of any right to the use of any of Lydia's money. Probably Lydia wanted to make sure Cotton did not take funds from her own inheritance to pay debts he owed her daughter.

In July 1721, Cotton wrote: "What very little Estate I had, has been sold, and the money is gone to pay my debts.... [M]y salary is not enough to support me comfortably...." He had even been forced to sell some of his clothes.

Cotton borrowed money from his son Increase (called Creasy), and got a scholarship for his son Samuel to attend Harvard. In April 1724, Cotton was threatened with a term in debtor's prison if he did not settle his financial affairs.

Lydia's temper had been erupting frequently during this troubled period, and Cotton continued to insist she was deranged. In his Puritan blindness, Cotton could only perceive the rightness of his own actions and could not or would not understand that Lydia had good reasons to explode in anger.

Another worry for Cotton was that his and Lydia's problems could have a negative impact on his church ministry. Apparently, they did not. On July 31, 1724, Cotton paid all his debts after the congregation collected a "love offering "of more than two hundred pounds sterling for him. His diary entry for the day read: "Inexplicable, inexplicably changeable, my wife has been restored to a new and healthy state. Her raging has abated. She embraced me with the highest ardors of love."

When the president of Harvard died in 1724, Cotton hoped with all his heart he would be named to be the new President. His father had been Harvard's president from 1685 to 1701, and Cotton felt he was now entitled to the position.

On August 12, 1724, however, Cotton was notified that another applicant had been chosen to head Harvard.

Cotton was desperate, and he probably asked Lydia for money to give to Harvard. He may have thought Harvard officials would reconsider their decision if he made a sizable contribution, or he may even have hoped the school would be renamed in his honor, as had happened to Elihu Yale.

Whatever happened between Cotton and Lydia, she became furious with him again and left him. He wrote on August 13:

> This night my unaccountable Consort, had a prodigious Return of her pangs upon her that seemed little short of a proper Satanical Possession. After a thousand unrepeatable invectives, compelling me to rise at Midnight, and retire to my Study that I might there pour out my Soul unto the Lord; she also got up in a horrid rage, protesting that she would never live or stay with me; and calling up her wicked Niece and Maid, she went

over to a Neighbour's House for a Lodging doubtless with numerous lies....

On August 23, 1724, he wrote: "In the evening of this day, my poor wife, returning to a right mind, came to me in my study, entreating that there might be an eternal oblivion of everything that has been out of joint, and an eternal harmony in our future conversations." He recorded that they prayed together, and that "the tokens of the greatest inamoration on her part ensured upon it."

Lydia returned home ten days after she left because she had learned that Cotton had been notified that his beloved son, Increase, was lost at sea. Since she knew of Cotton's deep affection for his son, she probably felt it was her duty to comfort him in his sorrow. From that time on, there were no other entries in Cotton's diary in which he complained about Lydia's paroxysms. During the next four years, he continued to minister to his congregation, even as warnings were given of dire events that were approaching.

In this last, Cotton had not misinformed them. There was a major earthquake in New England on October 29, 1727, and aftershocks continued until February 1, 1728.

People flocked to churches. Mather's church alone added 71 new members, more than the previous entire membership. Quakes occurring also in Europe and in the West Indies made it seem the earth might shatter into pieces.

Lydia nursed Cotton during his last illness, which lasted for five weeks. He died on February 15, 1728. She received one-third of his estate in a will he had made the year before his death.

An inventory of Cotton's estate revealed it to be valued at a total of 245 pounds. His household goods were meager, consisting of four old bedsteads, two old chests of drawers, two old tables, about 20 chairs (some of which were broken), a quilt, one candlestick, and so on. The most valuable items were silver plated tableware (cups, spoons, and so on) which were valued 121 pounds, five shillings and sixpence.

Lydia lived until 1734, dying on January 23. Her obituary in the *Boston News Letter* read: "Yesterday Morning died here Madam

Lydia Mather, the virtuous Relict of the late Reverend and Renowned Dr. Cotton Mather."

Bibliography

Bernhard, Virginia. "Cotton Mather's Most Unhappy Wife." Boston: *New England Quarterly*, September, 1987.

Silverman, Kenneth. *The Life and Times of Cotton Mather*. New York: Harper and Row, 1984.

Wendell, Barrett. *Cotton Mather: a Biography*. New York: Barnes and Noble Books, 1992.

5

HANNAH
CALLOWHILL PENN
(1671–1726)

A noted leader in the Quaker faith as an adult, William Penn was born on Tower Hill in London, England, on October 14, 1644. His father, also named William Penn, was an admiral in the British Navy who was knighted.

Young William attended school in Essex, and later went to Oxford University in 1660 to complete his education. University rules stated all students must attend the Church of England. When William, who believed an individual should have the right to worship as he chose, joined with other like-minded students to oppose the rule, he was expelled.

Admiral Penn then sent his son to France and Italy in an attempt to change his mind about religion. When he got back home two years later, young William did not mention religion, and his father sent him to London to study law.

In 1667 William went to Ireland to manage estates owned there by his father. In Ireland he met a Quaker minister named Thomas Loe, who converted William to the Quaker faith. William was jailed there for defending a meeting of Quakers at Cork when it was disturbed.

Quakers were held in low esteem by many people at the time and were ridiculed and often imprisoned. Admiral Penn was distressed by his son's decision, but he could not change his mind.

Quakers believe all humans have an Inner Light to guide them; they have no ordained clergy, no rituals and do not observe the sacraments. Quakerism (The Society of Friends) began as one of the nonconformist movements against the Church of England.

Young William Penn was put in prison in England several times over the next few years because of his beliefs and teachings. The first time, officials put him in the Tower of London, from which his father obtained his release. While in prison, William wrote a book entitled "No Cross, No Crown."

In 1669 he was jailed again when he refused to pay a fine imposed for his refusal to remove his hat at a court appearance. He was released in 1670 when his father died.

In 1671, he made a missionary tour with Friends to Europe, and the next year he married Gulielma Springett on April 4.

In 1677 Penn joined the Quaker leader, George Fox, and some other Quaker believers on another European tour. In conversing with his companions, he learned that their universal hope was to find a place to live where they could worship freely and without fear. Penn had been hearing about the New World developing in America and the unspoiled wilderness there. He decided that would be a good location for a colony of believers.

King Charles II of England owed William's father's estate about $80,000, and William asked the king to give him a charter for territory in America to pay the debt. On March 4, 1681, he received a charter for land between the New York and Maryland colonies, west of the Delaware River. His ruling power would be almost unlimited.

William's new project, which offered cheap land and religious freedom, attracted several thousand Quakers from England, Wales, Germany and Holland. He called his new project "Pennsylvania," which meant "Penn's Woods," the name suggested to him by the King's Council.

Penn drew up plans for the colony's government, which he dubbed the "Holy Experiment." He always paid Indian owners for their land, and neither he nor his colonists ever had trouble with any Indians.

In 1682, when Penn first visited his colony, he called a General Assembly into session at the Chester settlement in December, during which the Great Law, which guaranteed liberty of conscience, was adopted. Government employees had to express their belief in Christ, and court witnesses had to promise they would "speak the truth, the whole truth, and nothing but the truth."

Because the Dutch, German, and Swedish settlers who had reached the area earlier were growing food when Penn and his colonists arrived, there was no "starving time" in Pennsylvania.

In 1684 William returned to England to bring his family to join him. The centerpiece of his achievement was the city of Philadelphia, whose name means "City of Brotherly Love," from the Greek. In two years, 357 new homes were built there.

King James II was now on the English throne, and, as a Roman Catholic who knew religious persecution firsthand, he was sympathetic to William Penn. The King pardoned jailed Quakers, as well as other prisoners who had been jailed because of their religious beliefs.

In 1689 following the Glorious Revolution in 1688, however, Queen Mary and Prince William of Orange came to the English throne, having forced King James to give up his throne and go to the European continent to live. William Penn also lost control of his colony in 1692, when it was placed under royal control with a Benjamin Fletcher named royal governor.

In 1694, William's wife, Gulielma, the mother of his eight children, died. She never got to Pennsbury Manor, the house he had built in his colony. He did regain control of Pennsylvania that same year, however.

Pennsylvania had a government ruled by an elected assembly, but when problems arose with neighboring colonies in 1699, William was forced to return to his colony to solve the difficulties. He was soon eager to return to England and his children, however.

Back in England, he sought solace for his grief about his wife's death by attending Quaker meetings for worship. At one of the meetings, he encountered Thomas Callowhill, with whom he had been acquainted years before. Mr. Callowhill was accompanied by his young daughter, Hannah.

William was attracted immediately to young Hannah, but she was not accustomed to having men attracted to her so suddenly, and she was uneasy with William. He was almost twice her age and of a higher social rank, but he was heavily in debt. His deceased wife had brought a family fortune to their marriage, but Hannah did not have a fortune.

Hannah had been born on February 11, 1671, in Bristol in England, the daughter of Thomas and Anna Hollister Callowhill.

When Hannah remained cool to his advances, William began writing letters to convince her of his interest and love. His first letter said, "Let my letters have someplace, if I deserve any, though I hope Thou art sensible of me in that in which we can never be separated."

In another letter, he wrote,

> O let us meet here, most dear H! The comfort is unspeakable, and the fellowship indissolvable. I would persuade myself Thou art of the same mind, though it is hard to make Thee say so. Yet that must come in time, I hope and believe, for why should I love so well and so much, when I am not well beloved?

Even Letitia Penn, one of William's daughters, wrote to Hannah, saying her father's feelings for Hannah had been evident from the start of their acquaintance.

> I must tell Thee that at my father's first coming from Bristol, ten months since, though I kept it to myself, I perceived which way his inclination was going, and that he entertained an inward and deep affection for Thee, by the character he gave of Thee and the pleasure he took to recommend Thee as an example to others.

Letitia assured Hannah she would "be in enjoyment of Thy company, I promise myself, which I can truly say I prefer before any other settlement."

After a year of uncertainty, Hannah and William went before a Meeting of Friends in Bristol to request Quaker approval of their marriage. Their wedding took place in the old Broadhead Meeting

House in Bristol on March 6, 1696. William was 52 years old and a widower with teenaged children; Hannah was just 25.

Hannah's and William's first child died shortly afterbirth and was not named, but they had seven more children in the next several years. John was born in Philadelphia in 1700 and was called "the American" for that reason. Hannah, William and Letitia had returned to Pennsylvania in 1699, not long before John's birth.

After spending 23 months in Pennsylvania, the Penn family returned to England, where Thomas was born in 1702, Hannah Margarita in 1703, Margaret in 1704, Richard in 1706, Dennis in 1707 and another little girl named Hannah in 1708. Sadly, both babies named "Hannah" died early.

James Logan was a major help and influence in Penn's colonial project. Logan had been born in Ireland and came to Pennsylvania to be Penn's secretary in 1699. He worked to protect proprietary interests, and even served as acting governor from time to time as well.

Hannah Penn became acquainted with James Logan as well as other associates of her husband in the government of Pennsylvania while they lived there. The men became aware of Hannah's common sense, dignity and careful attention to details.

While in America, Hannah spent most of her time on their farm at Pennsbury, located in Bucks County, and she watched her husband become increasingly discouraged by his debts and the various political factions developing in the colony. When he proposed surrendering the Pennsylvania provincial government to the English Crown for a monetary settlement in 1703, Hannah did not oppose him in any way. She knew he had been imprisoned in 1688 for indebtedness.

He mortgaged the land at Pennsbury to an English Quaker group of trustees, retaining title to the property. The family had returned to England in 1701, but planned to come back to Pennsylvania and their Pennsbury estate soon, to rear their family. William left James Logan in charge of business affairs during his absence.

However, in 1712, both of Hannah's parents died, and William suffered multiple strokes, which paralyzed him. Hannah had to assume control of his business affairs. In fact, he was writing a letter to James Logan when his first stroke occurred. When Hannah found it, she sent it on to Logan.

Hannah was extremely busy for the next few years with managing her parents' estate, rearing their children alone and serving as administratrix of William's affairs. She and her children inherited most of his property when he died in 1718.

Hannah became ill in 1721 but she continued her contacts with the Pennsylvania colony, and she managed to workout an agreement with Lord Baltimore which defined the boundary line between Pennsylvania and Baltimore's Maryland colony, something that William had never been able to do.

Hannah died on December 20, 1726, at her son John's home in London, also of a stroke. She was buried beside William in Jordan' Friends Meeting Cemetery in Buckinghamshire.

On November 28, 1984, President Ronald Reagan conferred honorary citizenship on William and Hannah Penn. In Proclamation 5284, which was approved by the United States Senate, he wrote,

> In the history of this Nation, there has been a small number of men and women whose contributions to its traditions of freedom, justice, and individual rights have accorded them a special place of honor in our hearts and minds, and to whom all Americans owe a lasting debt. Among them are the men and women who founded the thirteen colonies that became the United States of America.
>
> William Penn, as a British citizen, founded the Commonwealth of Pennsylvania in order to carry out an experiment based upon representative government; public education without regard to race, creed, sex, or ability to pay; and the substitution of workhouses for prisons. He had a Quaker's deep faith in divine guidance, and as the leader of the new colony, he worked to protect rights of personal conscience and freedom of religion. The principles of religious freedom he espoused helped to lay the groundwork for the First Amendment of our Constitution.
>
> As a man of peace, William Penn was conscientiously opposed to war as a means of settling international disputes and

worked toward its elimination by proposing the establishment of a Parliament of Nations, not unlike the present-day United Nations.

Hannah Callowhill Penn, William Penn's wife, effectively administered the Province of Pennsylvania for sex years and, like her husband, devoted her life to the pursuit of peace and justice.

To commemorate these lasting contributions of William Penn and Hannah Callowhill Penn to the founding of our Nation and the development of its principles, the Congress of the United States, by Senate Joint Resolution 80, approved October 19, 1984, authorized and requested the president to declare these persons honorary citizens of the United States of America.

Even though they never realized their dream of returning to Pennsylvania, William and Hannah Penn still became citizens of the United States of America.

Bibliography

Faris, John T., *The Romance of Old Philadelphia*. Philadelphia and London: J. B. Lippincott, 1918.

Illick, Joseph E. *Colonial Pennsylvania, A History*. New York: Charles Scribner's Sons, 1976.

James, Edward T., Ed. *Notable American Women, 1607–1950*. Cambridge: Belknap Press of Harvard University Press, 1971.

Neidle, Cecyle S. *America's Immigrant Women*. New York: Hippocrene Books, 1976.

6

SYBILLA RIGHTON MASTERS
(1675–1720)

If Sybilla Masters was not the first woman inventor in America, she was one of the first. She was serious enough about her efforts to receive patents on her inventions from the British government.

Sybilla was born about 1676 in Bermuda to Quaker parents, William and Sarah Righton, the second of seven children. The Rightons emigrated with their family to Burlington in West New Jersey in 1687, where William Righton bought a plantation on the banks of the Delaware River that he named "Bermuda."

Sybilla first appeared in public when she testified as a witness for her father in the New Jersey courts in 1692. Some citizens of New Jersey, as well as some officials, did not like Quakers and would have seized their landholdings if they had dared.

Despite their opinions, Sybilla's father, both a merchant and a seaman, was a valuable asset to the area.

The West Jersey Society had been formed by Anglican businessmen to increase the exports of tar, timber and pitch; when these efforts were not successful, they turned their attention to land sales.

The West Jersey Council of Proprietors, composed entirely of Quakers, was organized in 1693 to protect Quaker landowners' interests.

When Colonel Daniel Coxe led the West Jersey Anglican group, in defiance of colony laws, to refuse to allow Quakers to vote so the

Anglicans could control land acquisition and sales, the Quaker proprietors were alarmed.

The government in England took control and ordered that Quakers could substitute an affirmation for an oath and continue to vote.

During this period, between 1693 and 1696, Sybilla married Thomas Masters, also a prosperous Quaker merchant and landowner who had come to Philadelphia in 1685 from Bermuda.

Masters had a fine house built for his family in 1702, on the riverfront in Philadelphia. It was described by James Logan, William Penn's secretary, as "the most substantial fabric in the town." Masters also built a summer home on a plantation he owned in the Northern Liberties of Philadelphia, which he named "Green Spring."

While Sybilla was busy running their household and rearing their four children—Sarah, Mary, Thomas and William—her husband was becoming politically active. He served as an alderman of Philadelphia, then mayor from 1707 to 1708, and then as provincial councilor from 1720 to 1723.

Sybilla turned her attention to inventions during this period. As many housewives have done when performing difficult chores, Sybilla decided there had to be a better way of pulverizing corn than grinding, and she would try to find it.

She had a long cylinder made of wood with projections on each side which caused a series of heavy pestles to drop onto mortars which were filled with kernels of corn. The corn was shelled and pulverized into finer grains than when it was ground by the usual method. Power was supplied to the procedure by either horses or a water wheel.

Sybilla was so pleased with her efforts, she told her Quaker meeting on June 24, 1712, that she wanted to go to London and get an official patent on her invention from the British government. The Meeting gave her a certificate of good standing to take with her.

On November 25, 1715, patent #401 was granted to Thomas Masters for "the sole use and benefit of a new invention found out by Sybilla, his wife, for cleaning and curing the Indian corn growing in the several colonies in America."

The end product was named "Tuscarora Rice" and was sold in Philadelphia stores as a cure for tuberculosis. While it has been termed "the first American patent medicine," it was really a food product, somewhat like hominy grits.

In 1714 Thomas Masters had bought "the Governor's Mill" on Cohocksink Creek which had originally been built for William Penn. Thomas planned to produce the corn product in large quantities, but when sales were light, he allowed the mill to go to other owners.

A few months later, on February 18, 1716, Sybilla was granted, also in Thomas's name, patent #403 for a method of staining and working with palmetto leaves to trim and make hats unlike any seen before in the colonies or in England. The official title was "Working and Weaving in a New Method, Palmetta Chip and Straw for Hats and Bonnets and other improvements of that Ware."

She obtained a permit for a monopoly on importing the leaves from the West Indies, and she opened a shop in London. It was called the "West Indies Hat and Bonnet," and she sold both items at prices beginning at one shilling, according to an advertisement in the *London Gazette* of March 18, 1716.

Sybilla also sold dressing baskets and baskets which could be used for children's beds, as well as matting for floors and furniture made from the palmetto leaves.

Sybilla returned home from England on May 25, 1716, as she missed seeing and being with her family. On July 15, 1717, Thomas Masters petitioned the Provincial Council to record and publish the patents in Pennsylvania and permission was given.

Sybilla died in 1720 in Philadelphia; Thomas died in 1723.

Bibliography

Tolles, Frederick B. "Sybilla Masters." *Notable American Women, 1607–1950.* Ed. Edward T. James. Cambridge: Belknap Press of Harvard University Press, 1971.

Vare, E.A. and Ptacek, G. *Mothers of Invention.* New York: Quill Press, 1987.

7

(BILHAH) ABIGAIL LEVY FRANKS
(1696–1756)

Abigail Levy Franks was one of the few Jewish women who came to live in colonial America of whom we have any record. She was born in London, on November 26, 1696, to Moses and Richa Asher Levy, one of their 12 children.

Her father, Moses Levy, was an Ashkenazi Jew, which meant his ancestors were from Eastern Europe or Germany. He came to America where he could worship freely without interference from government authorities. He was a ship owner and trader, and became a leader in the Jewish community in the New York colony where he and his family settled about 1700.

Mr. Levy had not suffered any real persecution for his religious beliefs in Europe, but he believed there would be greater economic opportunities in the New World.

However, it was comforting to him and his wife to know a synagogue had been established in New York City in 1682 in a rented house. The congregation was known as Shearith Israel (Remnant of Israel). It is the oldest Jewish congregation in America and is now in Central Park West in New York.

Mr. Levy was elected to serve as a constable in New York and was proud of the honor.

The original investors in the New Amsterdam colony (as New York was first called) were known as the Dutch West India Company, and some members of the company were of the Jewish faith. They had recruited actively among their fellow believers in Europe for colonists to go to the New World.

Jacob Franks was born in Germany in 1688, and he came to New York on the *Dove* in 1705. He had been living in England before he migrated and had brought some money with him to help him get established. He was also employed as a fiscal agent for England. He went to live with the Moses Levy family as a boarder upon his arrival in New York.

Abigail was nine years old when she saw Jacob for the first time, but a romance blossomed between the two young people as time passed. A marriage broker arranged their wedding in 1712 when Abigail was 16 years old.

Because she married at such a young age, Abigail was largely self-educated, chiefly through reading, but her education was advanced. Sometimes she erred in quoting literary works, but she had their meaning.

Jacob and Abigail had nine children, and became very wealthy after their marriage. They lived in the Dock area of the city, near the East River, in a large, elegant Dutch-style brick home. They also had a summer home in Flatbush. They entertained friends and business acquaintances often and lavishly.

Their first child was a daughter named Rachel (or Richa in Hebrew) for Abigail's mother. Rachel was followed by her brother, Naphthali, who was born in 1715; then Moses was born in 1718, David in 1720, a sister, Phila, in 1722, Sarah in 1731, Aaron in 1732, Rebecca in 1733 and a sister, Poyer, in 1734. Aaron and Sarah both died before their seventh birthdays.

Jacob Franks was named a freeman in New York in 1710, which meant he could vote in municipal and provincial elections and could hold office as a minor city official as well. However, neither he nor any other Jew could give evidence as witnesses in criminal trials.

New York was an interesting, diverse colony of traders, with more vibrant life and activities from the beginning than other colonies. Some of the freewheeling activities in the city were tolerated by the Dutch settlers because of their own more liberal attitudes about allowing people to differ in their beliefs, and some were inevitable because New York was the largest, most lively port in the New World.

With sailors coming ashore daily after spending long months at sea, there were few gloomy faces in the business trading area, and a variety of languages could be heard in the streets at any time. Prostitution flourished and tavern brawls were frequent, noisy and violent.

Abigail Franks complained about the noise generated by the hard-drinking gamblers, who were active day and night from Sunday night to Saturday morning in her neighborhood. However, if a visitor criticized New York, she defended her new home vigorously. She said there were fools in England too, and they were more pretentious.

Living in New York presented other problems because of primitive law enforcement, lack of sanitation and little fire protection. There were also the ever-present threats of yellow fever, smallpox and other diseases, which caused periodic epidemics.

Abigail and Jacob wanted their children exposed to cultural events, but theater and musical entertainments were infrequent, and if a family wanted regular exposure to such influences, they had to provide their own. The Franks children were taught to play the harpsichord and flute; some took singing lessons and some studied art.

Abigail deplored the lack of books available to colony residents. She really liked New York in many ways, but she considered both her Dutch and Jewish women neighbors to be "a stupid set of people."

There were newspapers available, starting in 1725 when William Bradford published the *New York Gazette*. It was a four-page edition which appeared each Monday, and was sold by subscription only. John Peter Zenger began publishing the *New York Weekly Journal* in 1733.

The news in either paper was not current, often several weeks old, but the papers carried business advertisements and the arrival and departure times of ships in the harbor.

The Franks family had a happy life together, but it was difficult to adhere strictly to their Jewish traditions. There was no ordained Rabbi in the region at first, and as late as 1791, a Jewish girl living in Richmond, Virginia, wrote to her family, still in Germany, "There is no Rabbi in all America to excommunicate anyone. This is a blessing here—Jew and Gentile believers are one. There is no galut (separation) here."

Abigail Franks was a devout Jew in her heart, and she and Jacob celebrated all Jewish feasts and holidays, as had their parents. When their oldest son, Naphthali, went to London to live in 1733, she wrote him, "You wrote me some time ago you was asked at my brother Asher's to a fish dinner but you did not go. I desire you will never eat anything with him unless it be bread and butter, nor nowhere else where there is the least doubt of things not done after our strict Judaical method, for whatever my thoughts may be concerning some fables, this and some other fundamentals, I look upon the observance conscientiously...."

Naphthali heeded his mother's advice and later married a girl of Jewish faith, as did his brother Moses, also living now in London.

There was less tension between the New York colony's inhabitants and the government in London between 1728 and 1748. New York did not send an official agent to represent it in England between 1730 to 1748.

In June 1731, however, the Duke of Newcastle sent a William Cosby to be New York's colonial governor, an unpopular choice. Abigail took an interest in the local political wrangles and she wrote Naphthali, "We have a perfect war here, and it is daily increasing, the Court being very much disliked. I think they are best that have nothing to do with him." She was referring to Governor Cosby.

Governor Cosby had incurred the wrath of locals when he deeded land in the Albany area back to the Indians. Chief Justice Lewis Morris and other landowners in Albany were outraged by his actions.

Abigail and Jacob remained neutral publicly in all the government disputes, and made an effort to keep peaceful relations with all their neighbors. She wrote Naphthali on May 7, 1733, "I confess

... it gives me a secret pleasure to observe the fair character our family has in the place by Jews and Christians."

On October 7 that same year, Abigail wrote him, "Moses is a-learning the mat(hemat)ecks at Mr. Mallcom's, who tells me he will go through it with abundance of ease and be perfect in very little time. Phila learns French, Spanish, Hebrew and writing in the morning, and in the afternoon she goes to Mrs. Brownell's. She makes a quick advance in what-ever she learns...."

The Mr. Mallcom mentioned by Abigail was Alexander Mallcom, a Scot who first set up a private school in New York in 1730, charging five pounds a year per student. When that income proved to be insufficient to support his family, he was hired to teach in the public school established in October 1732, by an Act of New York Assembly. Mallcom's brother, Quentin, also taught in both schools.

Abigail enjoyed gossip too. On June 5, 1737, in a letter to Naphthali, she said, "I am sensibly concerned at what happened in your Uncle Abraham's family with regard to his daughters, but its what I always expected for they will not consent to let them have husbands because the Jews with the best fortunes will not have them. So they can't blame them if they choose for themselves. I am really concerned for your uncle and wish him better luck with his other daughters."

Despite this, Abigail was shocked and deeply hurt when she learned that her own daughter, Phila, had secretly married Oliver DeLancey, a Gentile, the summer before.

Abigail had gone to stay in the family's summer home in Flatbush in 1742 because of a yellow fever epidemic, but Phila apparently stayed at home.

Peter DeLancey was a next-door neighbor of the Franks and his brother Oliver must have spent much of the summer there while he pursued his romantic liaison with Phila. They were married on September 8, 1742, before Abigail returned home. She did not learn of the marriage until sometime the next year.

Abigail wrote Naphthali, "I am now retired from town and would from myself (if it were possible to have some peace of mind from the severe affliction I am under on the conduct of that unhappy girl.) Good God, what a shock it was when they acquainted me she had left the house and had been married six months.... I had heard the report of her going to be married to Oliver DeLancey, but as such reports had often been of one of your sisters, I gave no heed of it further than a general caution of her conduct which had always been unblemished.... My spirits was for some time so depressed that it was a pain to me to speak or see anyone...."

Also in 1743, Abigail's son, David, now living and working in Philadelphia, married Margaret Evans, an Episcopalian. All of David and Margaret's children were baptized as Christians and married outside the Jewish faith.

Oliver DeLancey provided well for Phila and their seven children. He was a merchant and speculator in real estate. However, he was given to brawling when drunk, and in 1749 he was accused of stabbing to death a Doctor Colchoun.

One reason Phila and David married Gentiles may have been that they had few choices available for possible marriage partners. Abigail had made it clear to them that she held the few eligible Jewish possibilities in low regard.

On October 18, 1744, Abigail was beginning to wonder if she would ever see Naphthali again. She wrote him, "I don't know of anything I wish for but the happiness of seeing you, which I begin to fear, I never shall for I don't wish you here, and I am sure there is little probability of my going to England...."

Abigail's premonition was correct. She did not see Naphthali again after he had gone to London. She died in New York on May 15, 1756. She and Jacob had been married for 44 years. She was described as "the Amiable Consort of her husband" in the newspaper account of her death.

Jacob lived until January 16, 1769, when he died in New York City. He was buried beside Abigail in the Jewish cemetery on Chatham Square. His daughter Rachel was named to be the executor of his estate.

Naphthali, who had been the recipient of his mother's loving advice through the years, was a generous contributor to Jewish institutions and causes as long as he lived.

Bibliography

Dimont, Harry. *The Jews in America*. New York: Simon and Schuster, 1978.

Golden, Harry L. and Rywell, Martin. *Jews in American History*. Charlotte, N.C.: Henry Lewis Hartin, 1954.

Kammen, Michael. *Colonial New York: A History*. New York: Charles Scribner's Sons, 1975.

8

DEBORAH
READ FRANKLIN
(1708–1774)

Deborah Franklin was the wife of patriot and statesman Benjamin Franklin. She kept his business enterprise going and the home fires burning while Benjamin lived the good life in France and other European countries.

Deborah was born in 1708, probably in the Birmingham area of England. She was the daughter of John and Sarah Read, respected Quakers in the Birmingham community. They came to live in the Philadelphia area of the Pennsylvania colony in 1711.

They must have had substantial wealth, as Deborah's mother deeded valuable property to Deborah and her brothers a few years after John Read's death in 1724.

It was shortly before her father's death that Deborah met Benjamin Franklin for the first time. She was 16 years old and Benjamin was 18.

Benjamin had come to Philadelphia from his home in Boston, hoping to find work as a printer.

He had been walking around inspecting the neighborhood and got hungry. He stopped at a bakery and asked to buy some bread of a type familiar to him, but was told there was none available. Since at that time there was no central government in the colonies, money was different in each colony.

As he wrote later, he told the clerk to

give me threepenny worth of any sort. He gave me, accordingly, three great puffy rolls. I was surprised at the quantity, but took it, and having no room in my pockets, walked off with a roll under each arm and eating the other.

Thus I went up Market Street as far as Fourth Street, passing by the door of Mr. Read, my future wife's father; when she (Deborah) standing at the door, saw me and thought I made, as certainly I did, a most awkward ridiculous appearance.

Deborah admitted she was amused by the sight of a young man who appeared to be covered in bread.

It was hardly a propitious beginning for a romance, but a romance soon developed. When Benjamin was unable to find suitable affordable living quarters near the job he had been hired to do, Deborah's father agreed to let him rent a room in their house.

Deborah and Benjamin were soon considering marriage, but her father died about this time, and Sarah Read discouraged the couple from getting married for a while. She knew Benjamin was planning to leave Philadelphia soon to seek financing from his father in Boston to open his own printing business.

Mrs. Read may have felt it would be wise for Benjamin to get his business affairs arranged before he married, but the delay of their wedding would cause future problems.

Benjamin's employer, Samuel Keimer, in Philadelphia, was a man with odd religious beliefs, or so they seemed to Benjamin. Mr. Keimer would not cut his beard, he observed the Sabbath on Saturday, and he believed there should be no restraints on sexual adventures.

Keimer was 20 years older than Benjamin, and Benjamin probably viewed the older man as a sophisticate. It is a fact that Benjamin joined Keimer at least once in his erotic pursuits of pleasures with women.

All these activities and attitudes had their effect on Benjamin's feelings about his relationship with Deborah. She became aware that he now spoke vaguely of their marriage plans as being "someday."

Deborah was feeling uneasy, with reason. When Benjamin had

to make a business trip to London, he decided to end his relationship with Deborah. He wrote her a letter saying he liked London and had no intention of returning soon.

Deborah took the hint and turned her attentions in another direction. She was an attractive young woman, and she had no intention of waiting a lifetime for Benjamin to become an adult in his attitudes.

Deborah married a potter named John Rogers a few months later on August 5, 1725, but refused to live with him when she learned he had another wife.

Poor Deborah! She must have felt she had poor judgment about romantic matters.

Benjamin returned from London after about a year, and he returned to work for Keimer for a short time, until Keimer humiliated him in public.

After he stopped working for Keimer, Benjamin set up his own printing business, where he began printing the *Pennsylvania Gazette*. Keimer sold his printing interests to Benjamin, and from October 2, 1729, Benjamin's career with the enterprise continued for more than 30 years.

During these career changes for Benjamin, he and Deborah began seeing each other again. Old sparks rekindled and they set up housekeeping together on September 1, 1730, with no apparent objections from families or friends.

Truly, Deborah was uncertain about the status of her previous marriage to Rogers, who left to go to the West Indies after they separated, leaving behind a stack of unpaid bills. While a divorce or annulment was impossible with Rogers out of the country, Deborah made it clear that the marriage had ended for her; but the possibility of bigamy remained.

Neither Deborah or Benjamin felt any responsibility for paying Rogers' bills, so they had no formal marriage ceremony and Deborah became Benjamin's common-law wife.

Deborah was an heiress in a small way, and Benjamin may have felt her financial backing would aid in his own success. Also, Benjamin's unusual religious beliefs, not as radical as Keimer's, but different in their own way from conventional views, would not have been approved by Deborah's acquaintances, and she would have been shunned or "read" out of her Quaker Meeting.

Probably Benjamin loved her enough to want her not to be distressed by such results.

They had not been living together long when Benjamin brought his young son to live in their household. The little boy's name was William, and Benjamin cheerfully admitted that William was his illegitimate son. What he never revealed was the name of William's mother, and it is still unknown today.

Many people thought the child was Deborah's son, while others insisted he was a product of one of Benjamin's casual romantic liaisons. William was born on August 1, 1731, according to information in a letter written by Benjamin.

Whatever the truth of the matter, Deborah accepted the child, and the Franklins all settled into family life. Deborah helped Benjamin in his print shop, and everyone appeared to be contented and happy.

In 1732, Deborah's mother moved in with them. She and Deborah opened a shop in their home, where Sarah Read sold salves and ointments she mixed herself, and Deborah sold books and stationery. Deborah was pregnant with her first child.

Deborah and Benjamin welcomed their new son, whom they called Franky, on October 20, 1732, but he died of smallpox when he was only four years old.

Benjamin never recovered completely from his grief at the death of his little son, whom he had loved deeply. Many years later he wrote his sister, Jane Mecom, that his grandson (his daughter's child) "brings often afresh to my mind the idea of my son, Franky, though now dead 36 years, whom I have seldom seen equaled in everything and whom to this day I cannot think of without a sigh."

Sarah Franklin, called Sally, was born September 11, 1743 (new-style calendar date), and she lived to reach adulthood as did William.

Deborah complained at times that Benjamin loved William

more than he did either her or Sally, which could indicate William was not her own son. Daniel Fisher, who worked for Benjamin for a while, told of Deborah's unhappiness.

If William was the son of another woman, Deborah excelled in forgiveness of Benjamin's straying and in extending her affections to the little boy, for William loved Deborah dearly and always referred to her as his mother.

Benjamin's new venture, publishing *Poor Richard's Almanack*, brought him both fame and fortune. Throughout colonial America, the Almanack and the Bible were the two books almost certain to be found in every home.

Deborah was not well educated nor particularly brilliant in intellect, and she was content to live in Benjamin's reflected glory. She kept herself busy with their household and shop duties while Benjamin was busy somewhere else. He had been serving as postmaster in Philadelphia since 1737.

Benjamin had made friends over the years with many politicians, among whom was Alexander Hamilton, a highly regarded man of colonial affairs. It was probably through Hamilton's influence that Benjamin was named Clerk of the Colonial Assembly, the ruling body of Pennsylvania at the time.

From this post, Benjamin progressed further into political fields, which required him to be away from home for months and even years at a time.

While he was away, Deborah continued to perform her own duties faithfully and to attend Quaker Meeting. Her life was bound up with her children, Benjamin and her other relatives. Since she and Benjamin were trades people with no "old money" in their background, members of the official Philadelphia society took no notice of her.

In December 1757, Benjamin was again in London, and he asked his landlady there to help him shop for gifts for Deborah and Sally. The landlady, Mrs. Margaret Stevenson, did help him select cloaks, dresses, and other finery, which he sent home.

It was rumored in London by many of Benjamin's acquaintances that Mrs. Stevenson was a surrogate wife to Benjamin. If so, no hint was given to Deborah, but one of Benjamin's friends, a man named William Strahan, wrote a letter to Deborah, begging her to come to London to live with Benjamin.

He wrote:

> The ladies here consider him (Benjamin) in exactly the same light I do, perfectly agreeable.... Upon my word I think you should come over with all convenient speed, to look after your interest; not but that I think him faithful ... as any man breathing; but who knows what repeated and strong temptation may in time, and while he is at so great a distance from you, accomplish?

Most women who received such a letter would have begun packing a trunk immediately and making arrangements for a neighbor to feed the cat, but Deborah did not. She was afraid of the ocean voyage, and she wrote Mr. Strahan that she would not come.

Benjamin approved of her decision and wrote her on January 14, 1758, "I am sure there is no inducement strong enough to prevail with you to cross the seas.... Your answer to Mr. Strahan was just as it should be. I was much pleased with it. He fancied his rhetoric and art would certainly bring you over."

Whatever the attractions were in London, Benjamin did not return to Philadelphia and his family for five years.

Benjamin had retained his post as postmaster, however, and during his long absence Deborah ably carried on that business as well as in the print shop.

Deborah had a basic education, at least, as letters from her have been found, and she conducted Benjamin's and her own financial affairs. William Franklin succeeded his father as Clerk of the Assembly.

In November, 1762, Benjamin returned home, but he set about almost at once planning his return to England. He wrote his friend Strahan in December of that year, "In two years at the farthest I hope to settle all my affairs in such a manner as that I may then conveniently remove to England—provided we can persuade the good woman to cross the seas."

Strahan and Benjamin had hoped they might arrange a marriage between Strahan's son and Sally Franklin. However ,Deborah refused to allow Sally to go to England with Benjamin when he went back in 1765.

Benjamin had a new brick house built for his family while he was in Philadelphia, and Deborah told him she preferred to remain in it than go to England. He left without her in November 1764, and life went on for Deborah, Sally and William without Benjamin.

As for Sally's romantic life, she settled that herself when she married Richard Bache, a Philadelphia merchant, in October 1767. Mr. Bache had emigrated from England after Benjamin's return to Europe. Sally was 24 years old at the time of her wedding, and her groom was 30.

William Franklin feared Bache was a fortune hunter and he wrote Benjamin of his concern for Sally.

Benjamin felt he was too far away to interfere, so he wrote Deborah to judge whether the marriage was suitable. He cautioned her against planning an elaborate wedding because the construction of their new house had left him in reduced financial circumstances, but he said he would send Sally 500 pounds for her clothes and furniture.

When Sally and Richard had a son born on August 12,1769, they named him Benjamin Franklin Bache. Deborah attended the baby's christening at Christ Church in Philadelphia although her health was beginning to deteriorate.

William and his wife were the baby's godparents, and even William approved of the baby, writing Benjamin, "he is altogether a pretty little fellow, and improves in his looks every day."

With patriots in the American colonies beginning to resent the English government's onerous taxes on them, Benjamin found himself caught in the middle of the conflict. He wrote an article for the *London Chronicle* on November 8, 1770, explaining that the colonists were willing to pay some taxes but that they felt, they were entitled, in return, to have a voice in the way the money was collected and spent.

When the Stamp Act was passed by the English Parliament

colonists in America felt Benjamin had sold out his countrymen because he supported the measure. Deborah was on the spot in Philadelphia where she had to live daily with the taunts and insults from neighbors about Benjamin's errors in judgment.

The protests turned ugly. Deborah wrote Benjamin: "On Monday (night) last we had very great trouble.... Several houses were threatened to be pulled down. Cousin Davenport came ... stayed with me some time. Towards night I said he should fetch a gun or two as we had none."

She continued,

> I sent to ask my brother to come and bring his gun also, so we made one room into a fortress. I ordered some sort of defense upstairs such as I could manage myself.
>
> I said, when I was advised to remove, that I was sure you had done nothing to hurt anybody, I had not given offense to any person at all, nor would I be made uneasy by anybody, nor would I stir or show the least uneasiness—but if anybody came to disturb me, I would show a proper resentment.

Deborah began to wonder if she would ever see Benjamin again. It seemed he would never come home to stay. Her little grandson was a great blessing in her life, and she loved him dearly. Her pet name for the baby was "King Bird."

She wrote Benjamin frequent letters, telling him of the baby's development, so much that he teased her about her grandmotherly devotion.

When Mrs. Stevenson's daughter also had a son, Benjamin wrote Deborah about that baby. In February, 1773, he wrote her the little boy would not sit down to eat his breakfast unless "Pa" was called, which was the child's name for Benjamin.

Deborah must have felt dismay that Benjamin could become so involved with the child in England, when he had never even seen his own grandson and namesake.

During the months Benjamin continued his diplomatic negotiations with the British government in an attempt to prevent a war between England and the colonists, Deborah's health worsened. She told William that if Benjamin did not come home before winter in 1774, she felt she would never see him again.

Unfortunately, she was prophetic. On December 14, she suffered a stroke, died on December 18 and was buried on December 22, 1774. Benjamin did not even learn of her death until February 1775, but when he did, he made plans to leave England immediately.

Back in Philadelphia, Benjamin lived with Sally and her family. As errant husbands often do, he tended to idealize Deborah after her death. He remained involved in political affairs and was soon named to be a delegate to the Continental Congress when it met in Philadelphia.

William Franklin was now the colonial governor of New Jersey and a devout Loyalist, which caused Benjamin much unhappiness. Benjamin was a strong believer in the right of the colonists to seek their independence from British rule.

In February 1776, Benjamin resigned his Pennsylvania offices and, from that time on, devoted his life to peace conferences in an attempt to settle the serious disagreements between the English government officials and the colonists in America.

He went on to France, an ally of the American colonists, and spent several years negotiating peace treaties and trade agreements for the newly emerging United States.

Benjamin continued to give romantic attention to the attractive French women he encountered, and even proposed marriage to one; she refused him.

Benjamin returned to Philadelphia in 1786, where he was now honored by his fellow countrymen for his efforts in helping them gain their independence. He remained interested in developments in the new country and in its political affairs until his death on April 17, 1790.

Benjamin was buried in Christ Church cemetery beside Deborah.

Bibliography

Franklin, Benjamin. *Writings*. New York: The Library of America, 1987.

Meltzer, Milton. *Benjamin Franklin, The New American*. New York, London, Toronto, and Sydney: Franklin Watts, 1988.

Van Doren, Carl. *Benjamin Franklin*. New York: Viking, 1938.

Wright, Esmond. *Benjamin Franklin*. Cambridge: Harvard University Press, 1990.

Zall, P.M. *Founding Mothers*. Bowie, Md.: Heritage Books, 1991.

9

ANNA CATHERINE MAULIN ZENGER
(1718–1751)

Anna Catherine Maulin was born in the Rhenish Palatinate area of Germany in 1697 to Dutch parents. Her future husband, John Peter Zenger, was born in the same area that year, but his parents were Germans.

When both young people were 13 years old, they and their parents came to America, after enduring many hardships in Europe. The French army had invaded the area of Germany where they were born, and they went to live in the Netherlands in 1702 because the French did not approve of their religious beliefs and burned their crops and homes. Many other people left also.

After the refugees had endured five years of near starvation in the Netherlands, Queen Anne of England sent a fleet of ships to Rotterdam to bring about 30,000 of them to England.

They stayed in England for two years, but there were so many new arrivals that they could not find jobs to support themselves and their families. When the British government offered them free passage to America and money to help them get started, about 300 refugees asked to be allowed to go. Both the Maulin and Zenger families were included, and they reached New York in 1710 on a hot summer day.

Between 1708 and 1710, New York's governors Lovelace and Hunter brought more than 2000 of the Palatinate refugees to America, where the men could work in the lush pine forests, tapping the trees for resin to make tar and turpentine for use in building British ships. The governors were appointed by the King of England, King George II.

The Maulin and Zenger families had been on board the ship for 75 days, with insufficient food and water for all the 295 passengers. Thirty people died—John Peter's father being among them.

Rows of white tents had been erected in the New York field called the Common for shelter for the newcomers. Many tents were already occupied by earlier arrivals.

One problem facing young Peter Zenger was the need to get a job so he could support his mother, brother and sister. He asked William Bradford, a local printer, if he would take him on as an apprentice. Mr. Bradford agreed and Peter went to live with Bradford and his family.

Peter's brother was apprenticed to a carpenter. The mother found work as a nursemaid in a family with several children, and her little daughter was allowed to live with her there.

Anna Catherine's family followed the usual tradition of her father working while her mother stayed home with the children. Dutch women were allowed more freedom under the laws than English women, and Anna Catherine's mother may have regretted coming to America.

In Holland, a woman could own property in her own name, and could make contracts and take part in business in her own name alone. She could also make a will leaving her belongings to whomever she wished. An Englishwoman enjoyed none of these rights.

The Dutch women were as devoted to their homes and families as any women anywhere and were "goede vrouwen," for the most part.

From 1710 to 1718, Peter worked as an apprentice to Bradford and attended school at Andrew Clarke's Grammar Free School in the evenings.

When he reached the age of 21, Peter left Mr. Bradford's printing establishment and moved to Maryland where he opened a printing business of his own.

He soon married and had a son born in 1719. Unfortunately, his wife died before the baby reached his first birthday.

When Peter went back to New York in 1722 and asked Mr. Bradford for a job, Bradford hired him as a journeyman printer. Peter would do the same work as when he was an apprentice, but would now be paid.

On September 11, 1722, Peter married Anna Catherine Maulin. Catherine proved to be intelligent and a diligent worker, and she helped him realize his dream of being a printer when he became restless in his job with Bradford. He set up his own print shop on Smith Street in 1726, even though he had in 1725 become Bradford's partner in a newspaper, the *New York Gazette*.

The people living in the Albany area of the New York colony preferred to trade for furs with the Mohawk Indians in the Montreal area of Canada. The practice was a problem for the governors of the New York colony because they felt France, which controlled Canada, was exerting too much control in the fur-trading enterprise.

Governor Robert Hunter, who had been governor since 1710, tried to curtail the trading, without much success. When William Burnet was named governor in 1720, he was determined to stop it. However, he was unable to do so, and Governor John Montgomerie, who followed him, could not stop the trading either.

The Duke of Newcastle was given power by the King to name the next governor of New York, and he chose William Cosby, a relative of his wife.

Cosby arrived in New York Harbor on August 1, 1732, on the Seaford, a ship of the King's. Cosby's wife, two sons and two daughters accompanied him.

Rip van Dam, a member of the provincial council, had been acting governor for the past 13 months, and was liked by the people of New York. He had replaced Governor Montgomerie when the latter died.

Immediately upon meeting Governor van Dam, Cosby wanted to know how much he would be paid for the time he had worked prior to his arrival in New York. Van Dam explained his salary would begin upon his arrival, which displeased Cosby.

King George II ordered former Governor van Dam to share with Cosby the salary that Van Dam had received since the latter's appointment as governor. The New York Legislature had already paid Governor Cosby 8000 pounds for the work he claimed to have done before his arrival.

As the colony's official printer, William Bradford refused to print anything in his newspaper about Cosby and some of his outrageous actions, such as collecting money for Indians but never giving it to them, and refusing to give land to settlers unless he could keep one-third for his own use.

Peter Zenger thought such news should be printed in the newspaper, but William Bradford was paid by the British-controlled government, and he was afraid to insult the governor because he knew he could lose his own job.

Two important wealthy men in the New York colony were Lewis Morris, Jr., the son of New York's Chief Justice, and James Alexander, the best lawyer in New York. They also believed Governor Cosby's views of honesty were unusual, to say the least.

They came to Peter Zenger and asked him to print the facts about Governor Cosby, and they loaned Zenger money to set up his own printing shop.

One of Peter's first ventures was the printing of an unsigned pamphlet for Lewis Morris, Jr., which described government and governor problems. It sold well and got the citizens talking about political conditions. However, Zenger knew printing only such documents would not bring in enough money to support himself and his family.

He and Catherine decided to print books. Catherine learned to set type by hand, and how to sew the pages together and bind the books. She was also the shop manager.

Peter was not very successful as a book printer. He did not speak or spell English correctly, he was a slow worker and his book bindings looked like an amateur had done them. He lost business and had to take a job as a church organist for less money to pay their bills.

During this discouraging time, Zenger read in the *Pennsylva-*

nia Gazette that Benjamin Franklin was the new owner of that newspaper. The Gazette contained articles about disagreements between government officials, the kind of news Zenger believed should be made public. He and Catherine started selling the Gazette in their printing shop.

Peter wanted to publish his own newspaper, but he did not have enough money for such a venture. He and Catherine talked about Ben Franklin's paper and why it was so well received by the public. They decided it was the open, honest reporting of facts that made the difference.

Governor Cosby was by now suing former Governor Rip Van Dam for half of the money Van Dam had received as interim governor. Since Cosby knew a jury of New York citizens would not force Van Dam to pay, he convened a special court to hear the trial.

His actions alarmed Van Dam, James Alexander, Lewis Morris, Jr., and other like-minded citizens, who believed Cosby was rigging the court system to rule in his favor. The fact that he had not included Chief Justice Lewis Morris, Sr., indicated to them that he had no intention of allowing an honest and fair trial.

When Chief Justice Morris protested Cosby's actions, Cosby removed him from the office to which he had been elected by the citizens.

James Alexander and Lewis Morris, Jr., decided to form a new political party, which they called the Popular Party. They hoped to get Governor Cosby recalled to England or make him observe the laws already in place in the New York colony.

Lewis Morris, Jr., asked Peter Zenger to print a newspaper which would present their views to the people. James Alexander would be the editor, as he had more education than Zenger.

Peter Zenger remembered William Bradford's fear of arrest for articles he had printed in his newspaper in earlier years in which Bradford had criticized Quakers, and Peter hesitated. (In fact, Bradford's son had spent a short time in jail for some articles he had printed. The printer was legally responsible, not the writer.)

When an assemblyman died in Westchester County, the Popular Party asked Judge Morris to be their candidate for the office.

Judge Morris won by a vote of 231 to 151, and his son and other members of the party were encouraged in their campaign to get Governor Cosby recalled to England.

When Peter Zenger was convinced the public was largely in favor of the views held by the Popular Party, he agreed to start the publication of a newspaper to present the party's opinions. Catherine would be his assistant.

The *New York Weekly Journal* contained the election results and also mentioned that Quakers had not been allowed to vote, even when qualified. The newspaper's first edition appeared on November 5, 1733.

All the copies of the first-run edition were sold by nine o'clock that morning, and Peter and Catherine printed second and third editions.

The controversy quickly grew, with Governor Cosby having articles favorable to himself printed in the *Gazette* while the *Journal* printed such things as an account of Governor Cosby having three drunken sailors sign papers to get Van Dam arrested so Cosby could take all his property.

The sailors' captain was upset when he learned what had happened, and he ordered his men to go back to the official who had taken their affidavits, and admit they had lied.

Van Dam brought the information to Peter Zenger for his newspaper, and New York citizens were outraged. Governor Cosby had to drop his fabricated case against Van Dam.

When it came time to elect 14 aldermen in New York City, Governor Cosby's supporters brought in voters from other districts to vote for their candidates, but the Popular Party candidates won anyway.

Peter Zenger continued to publish unflattering but accurate reports about Governor Cosby, who had him charged with libel. Peter was arrested on November 17, 1734.

Peter's jail cell was cold, damp and dark, and infested with rats and insects. His jailers would not even allow him to have visitors until his friends told the jail officials that Judge Morris was getting ready to go to England where he intended to ask King George to recall Governor Cosby.

When they heard this, the jailers allowed Catherine to visit Peter. She told him that she and their sons would continue to publish the newspaper, and he could write articles and do some editing in his cell.

Catherine meant what she said. She bought paper and ink, set the type with a journeyman to help her, took care of the money matters and proofread articles before they were published. She wrote articles herself on European news events. The Zenger sons were willing helpers.

Peter's trial opened on July 29, 1735, with Chief Justice James DeLancey presiding. Andrew Hamilton, the most famous trial lawyer in the colonies, came from Philadelphia to assist Peter's court-appointed lawyer, John Chambers, in his defense of Peter.

Peter's lawyers admitted in court that Peter had printed the articles that criticized Governor Cosby, but argued that they would be libelous only if not true. The defense offered to call witnesses to verify that the information was true.

Judge DeLancey said none of that mattered. Peter had dared to criticize the Governor. Andrew Hamilton insisted every citizen had a right to express his opinions about the Governor and anyone else. They had a right of free speech in New York.

As Hamilton told the Judge and jurors, "It is not the cause of the poor printer, nor of New York alone, which you are now trying. It may, in its consequences, affect every free man in America.... It is the cause of liberty!!"

The jury returned a verdict of "Not Guilty," and Peter was freed from jail the next day.

Governor Cosby became ill a few months later and died.

Peter rested for several days before he resumed work on printing the City Charter. Following that, he printed a book containing all the legal documents about his own case. It was entitled "The Case and Tryal of John Peter Zenger."

As a record of the precedent for free speech, it was famous from the outset, and Peter's company subsequently printed several editions, a company in Boston printed two editions, and five were printed in England.

Peter continued to publish the *Journal* with the help of his family, and the New York Legislature named him Public Printer, as William Bradford was no longer able. The next year New Jersey also appointed Peter to be their public printer.

Peter Zenger died 11 years later on July 28, 1746, and Catherine again took charge and continued publication of the *Journal* with the information that it was "Printed by the Widow Catherine Zenger" for the next two and one-half years.

In 1748, John Peter Zenger, Jr., assumed full control of the business. He continued publishing the newspaper until March 18, 1751. Catherine and Peter had trained him well.

Catherine turned her attention to managing a bookshop until her death in 1751.

Bibliography

Kammen, Michael. *Colonial New York: a History*. New York: Charles Scribneer's Sons, 1975.

Westermann, Karen T. *John Peter Zenger*. Philadelphia: Chelsea House, 2001.

10

ANNE HENNIS BAILEY
(1742–1825)

Anne Bailey was an effective worker in several areas of life. She was a wife and mother and worked as a recruiter of men to fight hostile Indians and the British forces. She set up a delivery service to bring supplies to pioneer families when they needed them. She spent much of her life in raw, rowdy surroundings.

Anne Hennis was born about 1742 in Liverpool, England. Her father was a soldier in the Royal Army, and he named his baby daughter for Queen Anne.

There any claim to royal connections ended. Anne Hennis had no fortune to inherit and no one who wanted to introduce her to society. Anne was one of the common poor people in England who migrated to the colonies, hoping for a better life there.

Anne Hennis attended school in Liverpool in her early years, but when both of her parents died while she was still in her teens, Anne decided to come to America.

In 1761 Anne arrived in Staunton, Virginia, and lived there for a time with a family named Bell. She probably came as an indentured servant, by which means her employer would have paid for her passage.

While living with the Bells, Anne met a young frontiersman named Richard Trotter, and they fell in love. They were married in 1765 and went to live in Augusta County in Virginia, where their son William was born in 1767.

They led a contented, if hard, life. Richard enjoyed hunting, fishing and fur trapping, and Anne learned many survival skills from him which would prove valuable to her throughout her life.

Anne had an obsessive fear of Indians, as did many Europeans who had heard only bad stories about the violence and treachery of the native Americans. When impending Indian attacks on their village were rumored in 1774, Anne urged Richard to join the army and fight to keep the frontier and the settlers safe.

Richard had previously served in the colonial army during the Seven Years (French and Indian) War, in which British, Americans and Indians combined forces against French, Spanish and other Indian warriors.

Hard economic times had followed the Seven Years War and Britain had begun levying various taxes on the colonists to aid the English government. This time, however, Richard felt he would derive a direct benefit from protecting his own family, and he joined willingly.

A few months later, in a battle at Point Pleasant on the Ohio River in western Virginia, Richard Trotter was killed, and tradition holds that Anne saw the Indians kill him.

Whatever happened, Anne was left a widow at age 32, with a small son to rear alone. Her dislike and distrust of Indians increased.

Possibly it was occasioned by guilt feelings because she had urged Richard to rejoin the army, but Anne became an ardent recruiter of other men to fight Indians.

Anne left her young son in the care of a neighbor, Mrs. Moses Mann, and traveled on horseback from the Potomac River to the Roanoke River in her recruiting efforts.

She was unflagging in her zeal to find men to fight, and when the British invaded the colonies and the Revolutionary War started, she had no thought that she was recruiting men to fight her own countrymen as well as Indians. America had become her home.

It was during this period that Anne adopted what she considered to be a practical mode of dressing—buckskin pants, a man's coat, heavy work shoes, a belt at her waist which held a hunting knife, and a man's hat on her head. She carried a rifle on her shoulder.

Anne may have deliberately tried to make herself unattractive to protect herself from men's unwanted advances. She had to earn a living, after her husband's death, for herself and her son, so she became an official messenger from Staunton, Virginia, to various outlying Army forts. She carried letters, ammunition and other needed supplies all during the Revolutionary War.

Anne was often on her horse for two or three days at a time, as the distances between points she serviced ranged from about 40 miles to 120 miles.

Along the way, Anne made camp at night and often shot small game for food. She located a fair-sized cave near her customary route, in which she often took shelter, especially in severe weather, or when the Indian threat was worse than usual.

The Indians did not know what to make of this odd woman who rode fearlessly through the forests, camped alone on the trail and had no companions. Some Indians thought she was insane and thus under the protection of the Great Spirit. Others believed she had a special magic she would use to hurt them if they bothered her. She was known to all as the White Squaw of the Kanawha.

On November 3, 1785, Anne remarried. Her new husband, John Bailey, was also an Army scout and border soldier. They were married in Lewisburg, in a part of the Virginia colony which is now West Virginia. The Reverend John McCue was the officiating minister. Anne was now 43 years old.

In 1788 John Bailey was transferred to the new Fort Lee at the present-day site of Charleston, West Virginia, and he and Anne went there to live.

Anne got a job serving as a regular courier for the Army on a route between Fort Lee and Point Pleasant's Fort Randolph, a distance of 60 miles one way.

Again, she had to be self-sufficient. She carried an axe and if she needed wood, she cut it. If she needed food she shot wild game, which she roasted on a stick over her campfire.

In 1790, Colonel George Clendenin, commanding officer at Fort Lee, received a message that the Indians were about to begin attacking all along the Kanawha River. He posted sentries on alert and made all the preparations he could.

In January 1791, word came that an army of Indian warriors was approaching Fort Lee. Colonel Clendenin checked his supply of gunpowder and found it was dangerously low. He was afraid it would not be enough to last through a sustained attack of several days by the Indians.

The colonel asked for a volunteer to go to Lewisburg, about 100 miles away, to get more gunpowder.

When no soldier stepped forward, Anne told the colonel she would go, and she did. She brought the gunpowder back in time to save the fort from destruction by the Indians. In gratitude, the soldiers at the fort gave her the black horse she had ridden on her mission.

Anne named her new mount "Liverpool," in honor of her English birthplace.

Her husband remaining in the Army, Anne set up a delivery service for the people living between Point Pleasant and Staunton, Virginia. She drove cattle and other livestock including one order for 20 geese.

Colonel Clendenin, her husband's superior officer, had ordered the geese but refused to pay Anne when she brought only 19. She had traveled about 100 miles, but to the colonel that was no excuse.

Anne reached down into her saddlebag and brought out a dead goose and threw it at the colonel's feet. He paid her then.

Anne's soldier husband, John, was murdered in October,1794, reportedly by a fellow soldier.

When the Treaty of Greenville ended hostilities with the Indians, in 1795, Anne lost her job as an Army courier, and she went to live with her son, who was now married and had a family. His home was at Point Pleasant, and Anne stayed with him and his family for three years. She enjoyed the hunting and fishing which abounded in the area, but eventually she decided to go back to work and earn her own keep.

Since she had worked as a messenger and courier for the Army and later had her own delivery service, Anne decided a pony express delivery service was a natural. She established a regular service between Staunton and Gallipolis on the Ohio, transporting to the border settlements anything she could carry on horseback, such as letters, medicines and other small packages of all kinds.

Occasionally, she drove cattle and hogs between the settlements. On these occasions, she walked part of the way.

Anne still loved her horse, Liverpool, and she always fed and curried him herself when she stopped at a wayside inn to spend the night. One of her favorite inns along the way was known as the Alexanders.

According to statements by her contemporaries, Anne was short in stature, but sturdily built and muscular. She was an intelligent woman and could read and write. She enjoyed telling stories of her adventures, and often moved her listeners to tears.

Anne modified her bizarre costume for her delivery service, wearing a linsey-woolsey dress instead of men's pants. She covered her unkempt gray hair with either a hat or a large kerchief, folded into a three-cornered shape and tied under her chin.

Anne was accommodating to the settlers she encountered in her travels, and would willingly help repair a fence or carry water for a settler in need. She had a strong sense of humor and loved practical jokes, even when she was the target of the joke.

Once, Anne encountered some Indian braves while on a delivery mission, and she rode Liverpool at a fast pace until she found a hollow log to conceal her. While she was in the log, the Indians stole her horse. When night came, Anne followed their trail to the Indian camp, grabbed Liverpool's reins, mounted and rode safely away into the darkness.

In 1818, Anne's son, William Trotter, bought a farm in Gallia County, Ohio, and assumed his mother would move there to live with him and his family. However, Anne refused to leave the Kanawha River area, and she built a rude house for her home, using fence rails.

Anne's age was slowing her down, however, and William sent his daughter to stay with her. After a few months, Anne moved to a house in Ohio that William had built for her.

Anne always loved children. If she saw young boys wandering around in her neighborhood on Sunday, she believed they ought to be in church, and she would take them to her cabin and teach them to read the Bible. Since she still won prizes in local shooting matches, the little boys probably did not need much persuading.

William Trotter and his wife had a total of ten children. One daughter, Mary, married James Irion, and they had 12 children. Mary's son, John, had two sons whose names were Brooks and Harry Irion. Brooks was a long-distance runner who once raced for 50 miles. Harry was an attorney for the United States Forest Service until he retired in 1951.

On November 22, 1825, Anne died in her sleep at the age of 83. Two of her granddaughters were with her. In her obituary in *The Gallia Free Press* on December 3, 1825, the account said she was more than 100 years old, but all official records indicated she was in her early eighties. She was buried in the Trotter graveyard.

The Daughters of the American Revolution organization had Anne's body exhumed in 1901 and re-interred at Point Pleasant. In one of the DAR's annual reports, printed in 1905 by the Government Printing Office, the following account appeared:

"The ashes of Anne Bailey, the scout, who belonged to General Andrew Lewis's Army were taken up from where they had long been buried ... and placed alongside the soldiers she had so faithfully served, many times at the risk of her own life."

Anne's first husband, Richard Trotter, was one of the soldiers mentioned.

A monument was placed at Anne's grave in 1925 by Captain C.C. Bowyer, President of the Merchants National Bank of Point Pleasant. A bronze plaque on the marker reads:

Ann Hennis Trotter Bailey
Revolutionary Scout
Born in Liverpool, England, 1742
Died 1825
Colonel Charles Lewis Chapter, D.A.R.
1925.

Bibliography

Cook, Robert Bird. *The Annals of Fort Lee.* Charleston: The West Virginia Review Press, 1935.

Ellet, Elizabeth F. *The Pioneer Women of the West.* Philadelphia: Porter and Coates, 1873.

Lewis, Virgil A. "Anne Bailey, The Pioneer Heroine of the Great Kanawha Valley," Point Pleasant, W. Va.: *The State Gazette*, 10–10–1901.

11

MARY JEMISON
(1743–1833)

Mary Jemison was born in 1743 on board a ship, the *Mary and William*, which had left Ireland a few weeks earlier. Her parents, Thomas and Jane Erwin Jemison, were emigrating with their other three children to the colony of Pennsylvania, where they hoped to achieve a higher standard of living.

The ship docked at Philadelphia, and after spending a short time in that city, Thomas moved his family to Adams County, Pennsylvania, near Gettysburg.

Their life was hard, but the two older sons, John and Thomas, worked, as did the older daughter, Betsey. As baby Mary began to grow up, she, too, was assigned household and farm chores, including field work when needed. When two more sons, Robert and Matthew, joined the family in a few years, the Jemisons moved to a larger farm.

Mary matured into a normal adult, but she was always unusually small in stature, with light brown curling hair, blue eyes and a fair complexion. She studied willingly the lessons her mother taught her and embraced the religious beliefs of her parents.

Early on one spring morning in 1758, when Mary was 15, an Indian war-whoop sounded in the nearby woods, which was immediately followed by shots, and then a chorus of whoops. Mary's mother was cooking breakfast and her father was mending an axe handle in the yard. John and Thomas were in the barn, and they hid when they heard the commotion. They survived the raid, but Mary never saw them again.

There were four Frenchmen and six Seneca Indians in the raiding party, and they captured the Jemisons, except for the two sons, and rushed their captives back to the Indian camp for the next two days, fearing pursuit. Mary's mother tried to encourage the other captives, and she begged them to remember their religious beliefs.

Mrs. Jemison cautioned Mary to "Remember my child your own name and the names of your father and mother. Be careful not to forget your English tongue. Don't forget the prayers I have learned you, and say them often. Be a good child and God will bless you."

On the second night after their capture, Mary was given moccasins to wear instead of her shoes, as was a neighbor boy who had been captured in the same raid. Mary's mother told her it was a sign Mary and the boy would be spared, but the others would be killed the next day.

Mrs. Jemison was right. Both of Mary's parents were killed, as were her sister, Betsey, and the two younger Jemison sons.

When Mary and her captors finally reached the Indian camp, Mary was assigned to stay with two Seneca Indian women who would be her "sisters." The women were kind to Mary, and as they traveled around, Mary's protectors made sure she had only light work to do.

Time passed and Mary tried to fit into Indian life. She dreamed of going back to white settlements, but she knew there was no one to ransom her. Her Indian sisters would not allow her to speak English and she dressed as an Indian.

After a few weeks, the Indian women told Mary they were leaving her to go back to their home tribe. Mary would become the squaw of Sheninjie, an Indian of the Delaware tribe who had recently come to the camp.

Mary said later she had feared for her life, but she had never expected to be a wife to an Indian. However, she was a captive and had to do as she was told. Soon she had a little daughter, who died shortly after birth. Some months later she had a son, whom she named Thomas after her father.

Early that winter Mary was sent to join her Indian sisters at the permanent Indian camp at Geneshaw, located on the banks of the Genesee River further north. Sheninjie went part of the way with her, but turned back to hunt with the other braves. When Mary arrived at the camp, her "sisters" seemed glad to see her and her baby. An older Indian woman was named to be Mary's "mother."

When spring came, Mary worked in the fields with the Indian women as one of them. The Senecas were good farmers and Mary was never hungry. She enjoyed the chatter of the women as they worked and found she was even hoping Sheninjie would return.

In July news came to the camp that Sheninjie had died. Mary said, "Strange as it may seem, I loved him," when she recounted her adventures in later years to her biographer, Dr. James Everett Seaver.

As more time passed, Mary was realizing she would probably never return to live with white people, and she wondered how she would manage without her Indian brave.

Mary tried to adapt completely to Indian ways, but there were some customs she could not accept. She would not drink their liquor, which they drank to great excess, and she would not dance at their celebrations.

By now, however, Mary felt a closeness to the Indians and identified with them through her child. When a Dutch trader visited the camp and offered to take her to an English village, she refused and hid until he left camp. No one would have stopped her leaving this time.

When little Thomas was about three years old, Mary took another Indian husband, named Hiokatoo. Although he was always good to Mary, his cruelty to prisoners was beyond belief. She said he enjoyed inflicting pain and watching pain being inflicted by others.

Hiokatoo was 60 years old when they married, but he was in excellent health, and would live to be 103 years old. They had a total of six children and lived together for more than 40 years.

Their oldest son, John, inherited his father's blood-thirsty tendencies and murdered both his brother, Jesse, who was gentle and loving, and Mary's first son, Thomas, who made the mistake of referring to John as a witch.

All three of the young men were alcoholics, and Mary detested the habit. John himself was murdered five years later.

By now, Mary had developed a bitterness toward white people, who, she felt, were debasing Indians with liquor and by their attempts to convert them to Christianity. Mary said Indians should be left alone to be Indians.

Mary had three daughters still living, and during the Revolutionary War when the British burned their Indian village to the ground, Mary and the Senecas fled the area. The British had hoped the Indians would join forces with them if their homes and food were destroyed, and it did work out that way.

Mary and her children went about seven miles south, where she found employment with two runaway slaves in harvesting a large corn crop, for which she received a portion in payment. When the slaves moved on with their profits from the crop, Mary took the farm for her own home, and in 1780 she built a shack to house herself and her children.

Here, on Gardeau Flats, she and her children farmed for the next few years. She bought some cattle. The land here was black and fertile and Mary prospered. Apparently Hiokatoo spent most of his time hunting and was gone from home much of the time.

After the Revolutionary War, land developer Robert Morris and others came to the area to buy Seneca land. Morris brought trinkets for the Indian women and "firewater" for the men.

That week in 1797 was a great week from the viewpoint of the Indians. Mary was not as taken in by the white speculators as the Senecas were, and she insisted on retaining title to the land on which she had lived for many years. The Senecas agreed that it was Mary's land and ratified her claim to it.

Mary was 54 years old, aging and somewhat grotesque in her appearance, wearing her combined items of Indian and white women's clothing. She wore buckskin moccasins, a petticoat, a coat fastened with leather thongs and a most disreputable-looking hat on her head.

Morris did not take Mary's claim of ownership of the land too seriously. He was tired and wanted to settle the matter completely.

What did a woman know of business, and, anyway, how much cropland could Mary hope for? It was all so vague. She was just a strange little woman who wanted to feel important, he thought.

After Morris also ratified Mary's claims, he discovered he had ceded almost 18,000 acres of the best land along the Genesee River to Mary. There was no way he could change the deal.

By 1804 white men had cleared Indian land that Morris had obtained and then resold to settlers, and were farming it. Woodland trails had become roads and bridges were spanning streams. The old way of life was ending for the Senecas, and many left the area to move further into the wilderness. In later years, white settlers would follow them there, too.

In 1823, Mary found she could no longer supervise the care of her extensive acres, and she sold all her real estate to Jellis Clute and Micah Brooks, with the exception of a homesite a mile wide and two miles long. She meant to leave this property to her children when she died, but instead, in 1831, she left her land on the Genesee to go to live on the Seneca reservation near Buffalo, New York.

Two years later she became very ill and reverted to her childhood Christian faith when the Reverend Asher Wright, a Protestant missionary, prayed the Lord's Prayer with her. She remembered her childhood, her parents and her childhood home. She was buried on the reservation with a Christian funeral service.

Years later, her coffin was moved to Letchworth State Park, above the Genesee, where she rests today. Her grave is marked by a bronze statue on a marble monument, which shows the young Mary who was captured by the Indians. The grave is located on property she once owned.

Mary was a brave woman who endured and triumphed under conditions most could only imagine. She deserves her place in history.

Bibliography

Berkin, Carol. *First Generations: Women in Colonial America*. New York: Hill and Wang, 1996.

Clune, Henry W. *The Genesee*. New York: Holt, Rhinehart and Winston, 1963.

12

ELIZABETH HUTCHINSON JACKSON
(1747–1781)

When Elizabeth Hutchinson Jackson and her husband, Andrew, left Carrickfergus in County Antrim in Ireland in 1765 it was with the hope of finding a better life for themselves and their children in the Carolina colonies. Their two sons, Hugh, age two, and Robert, an infant, sailed with them to the New World.

Andrew Jackson had been working as a tenant farmer in Castle-reagh on the northeast coast of Ireland, so when he and his family reached the Waxhaw area in South Carolina, he was ready and willing to begin the task of clearing land for his own farm and building a cabin to house his family.

The Jacksons settled on a 200-acre tract of land located on the dividing line between North Carolina and South Carolina, which was near some of Elizabeth's sisters and their families, who had emigrated earlier. It seemed possible that life might become better when Andrew harvested his first crop.

The Jacksons were typical of the Scotch–Irish immigrants to the region, who were also refugees from religious oppression by the Church of England. Many of them were weavers, whose cottage industries were rendered unprofitable by English laws prohibiting importation of Irish goods.

These people were rugged pioneers who wanted to own their property free and clear. They were accustomed to hard work, and they labored willingly to clear the cheap land they bought for farming.

Their homes were made of hand-hewn logs notched together at the four corners, the spaces between the logs filled with mud, and bear-greased paper in the window openings for privacy. Fireplaces were used for heating and cooking.

The men wore deerskin breeches and homespun shirts made by their wives, and the women and children wore clothes made from cotton or wool which was spun into thread on spinning wheels and woven into cloth by the women on handlooms.

There was ample food in the New World, consisting of hog meat, hominy grits made from corn, fish, wild turkeys and partridges, rabbits and squirrels, supplemented by vegetables from their own gardens. A flock of chickens provided eggs and the family cow or cows provided milk and butter. Women and girls usually worked alongside the men in the fields.

They were eager participants in politics, and often barbecued whole oxen for refreshments at political rallies. They had less interest in pursuing the development of a central government to control their lives than in local regulation by county or regional officials.

Their entertainments included clan gatherings, shooting matches, quilting bees and barn "raisings," where all the men and boys joined together in helping a neighbor build a barn. Women furnished food for the hungry workers and gossiped as they worked.

Sadly, in March 1767, Andrew Jackson died suddenly after lifting a heavy log, leaving Elizabeth, pregnant with a third child, with two young sons to rear alone.

Elizabeth took her two little boys to visit her sister, Jane Crawford, and her family who lived in nearby South Carolina. Three days later, while still at the Crawford home, Elizabeth gave birth to her third son, whom she named Andrew for his deceased father.

Elizabeth Jackson must have felt her dream of a better life had ended with the death of her husband. How could a widow with three small sons manage even to survive?

The answer to her problem lay with the Crawfords. Jane Crawford's health was poor, and she wanted Elizabeth to move in with her and her family. Of course, she indicated the Jackson children were welcome too. The Crawfords had eight children of their own, and living conditions must have been very crowded, with some children required to "sleep at the foot of the bed."

Young Hugh Jackson spent time at intervals with another uncle living in North Carolina, to help with the crops, but Elizabeth, Robert and Andrew lived with the Crawfords for some 12 years.

Andrew was very bright and learned to read at age five, when a local pastor, Dr. William Humphries, gave him a few lessons. Like most Scots, Elizabeth was a devout Presbyterian and she had hoped Andrew might study for the ministry, but she had not considered his exuberant, rollicking nature. Andrew had inherited Elizabeth's red hair and blue eyes, but not her devotion to religious matters.

Even with her multiple household duties, Elizabeth took time to be a real mother to her own sons. She told them of the bravery of their grandfather during the siege of Carrickfergus in Ireland by the English forces years earlier. They listened with rapt attention as she explained how oppression by the English nobility led to uprisings by the poor common people and to fighting in Ireland.

When the American Revolutionary War began, the Jackson boys were already enemies of the British forces. Hugh died in a battle at Stono Ferry of "excessive heat … and the fatigues of the day."

When the war moved on to Waxhaw, Andrew and Robert went with American patriots on fighting forays. The troops were led by Colonel William Richardson Davie. Andrew eagerly absorbed the strategies and tactics employed by Colonel Davie and developed the ideas he would use later as Major General Jackson in the War of 1812.

Andrew and his brother were captured in August 1780,and put in a British military prison in Camden, South Carolina. Both boys contracted smallpox, and when Elizabeth rode 40 miles on horseback to plead for their release, it was granted. She arranged for five neighbor boys to be released at the same time in exchange for the release of 13 British soldiers.

Elizabeth could only get two horses to use to bring her sons back home. She put Robert, who was obviously dying, on one of the horses, and she rode the other back to Waxhaw. Andrew and the neighbor boys walked the 40 miles, part of the way in a cold winter rain.

Robert died shortly after reaching Waxhaw, and Elizabeth had to give Andrew several weeks of devoted nursing care to help him recover. It was several months before here gained his full strength.

Meanwhile, Elizabeth learned that some of her Crawford nephews were being held prisoner on board British ships in the Charleston harbor and that they were ill with cholera. She and two of her nieces set out on horseback to travel the 160 miles to Charleston to nurse their kinsmen back to health.

They did what they could for the prisoners, but Elizabeth fell victim to the cholera epidemic, and died within a few days after reaching Charleston in 1781. Andrew received a small package of her personal belongings after she had been buried in an unmarked grave with other victims of the cholera.

Andrew was devastated by the death of his courageous mother. He told a friend of her final words to him before leaving for Charleston:

"Andy, never tell a lie, nor take what is not your own, nor sue … for slander. Settle them cases yourself."

Andrew was the only member of his immediate family left and he was now 14. Many years later he would be elected president of the United States, the first president to be elected from the ranks of the common people. On the day of his inauguration, he must have wished his mother and father could have been present to share his triumph. He also mourned his wife, Rachel, who had died in December 1828, three months earlier.

Elizabeth had done her work well with Andrew. He was a brave, loyal American, who served his country with distinction.

Bibliography

DeGregorio, William A. *The Complete Books of United States Presidents.* New York and Avenel, N.J.: Wings Books, 1993.

Whitney, David C. *The American Presidents.* Garden City, N.Y.: Doubleday, 1985.

13

PHILLIS WHEATLEY
(1753–1784)

Phillis Wheatley was a black woman slave in the Boston colony before the Revolutionary War, but her status did not prevent her from becoming the first significant black author in her new country.

Phillis was born on the Gold Coast of Africa, probably in the Senegal–Gambia region, about 1753. She came to America on the ship Phillis, and arrived in Boston on July 11, 1761. She would write a poem, *On Being Brought from Africa to America* later on in life, in which she explained her belief that she gained more than she lost by being brought to America.

Phillis was a frail little girl of seven, when Susanna Wheatley, the wife of Boston merchant John Wheatley, bought her from a Boston slave dealer. Phillis went to live in the Wheatley home on King Street in Boston, originally as an attendant to Mrs. Wheatley.

The Wheatleys had twin children, Mary and Nathaniel, who were 18 years old when Phillis joined their household. Mary Wheatley took Phillis as her personal project, to educate and to teach her religion.

Phillis must have been highly intelligent for she was soon learning English, both the language and literature, Latin, history, geography and the Bible. Within a few years she had as broad an education as most white women in Boston. She began writing poetry when she was 12 years old. Her poems were reminiscent of those of Alexander Pope and Thomas Gray.

Phillis Wheatley

Her first poem was written in 1765.

*To the Reverend Doctor Thomas Amory on Reading His Sermons
on Daily Devotion, In which Duty is Recommended and Assisted:*

> To cultivate in ev'ry noble mind
> Habitual grace, and sentiments refin'd
> Thus while you strive to mend the human heart,
> Thus while the heav'nly precepts you impart,
> O may each bosom catch the sacred fire,
> And youthful minds to *Virtue's* throne aspire!
> When God's eternal ways you set in sight,
> And *Virtue* shines in all her native light,
> In vain would *Vice* her work in night conceal,
> For Wisdom's eye pervades the sable veil.
> Artists may paint the sun's effulgent rays,
> But *Amory's* pen the brighter God displays:
> While his great works in *Amory's* pages shine,
> And while he proves his essence all divine,
> The Atheist sure no more can boast aloud
> Of chance, or nature, and exclude the God;
> As if the clay without the potter's aid
> Should rise in various forms, and shapes self-made,
> Or worlds above with orb o'er orb profound
> Self mov'd could run the everlasting round.
> It cannot be—unerring *Wisdom* guides
> With eye propitious, and o'er all presides.
> Still prosper, *Amory*! still may'st thou receive
> The warmest blessings which a muse can give,
> And when this transitory state is o'er
> When kingdoms fall, and fleeting *Fame's* no more,
> May *Amory* triumph in immortal fame,
> A noble title, and superior name!

Her second poem was written in 1767 for a grandnephew of
Susanna Wheatley, who was then a student at Cambridge. His name
was Thomas Wallcut.

To the University of Cambridge, Wrote in 1767

While an intrinsic ardor bids me write
The muse doth promise to assist my pen.
'Twas but e'en now I left my native Shore
The sable Land of error's darkest night
There, sacred Nine! for you no place was found,
Parent of mercy, 'twas thy Powerfull hand
Brought me in Safety from the dark abode.
To you, Bright Youths! he points the heights of Heavn,
To you, the knowledge of the depths profound.
Above, contemplate the ethereal Space
And glorious systems of revolving worlds.
Still more, ye Sons of Science, you've receiv'd
The pleasing Sound by messengers from Heav'n,
The Saviour's blood, for your Redemption flows.
S(ee) Him, with hands stretch'd out upon the Cross!
Divine compassion in his bosom glows.
He hears revilers with oblique regard.
What Condescention in the Son of God!
When the whole human race, by Sin had fal'n;
He deign's to Die, that they might rise again,
To live with Him beyond the Starry Sky
Life without death, and Glory without End....
Improve your privileges while they Stay:
Caress, redeem each moment, which with haste
Bears on its rapid wing Eternal bliss.
Let hateful vice so baneful to the Soul,
Be still avoided with becoming care;
Suppress the sable monster in its growth,
Ye blooming plants of human race, divine
An Ethiop tells you, 'tis your greatest foe
Its present sweetness turns to endless pain
And brings eternal ruin on the Soul.

Phillis was in contact daily with well-educated, cultured, Christian citizens, and it was inevitable that she would adopt their views and morals.

Susanna Wheatley was impressed by the young girl's poetic ability. She assigned only light household work to Phillis and became an ardent promoter of the publication of her poems.

It is greatly to her credit that Phillis did not take advantage of her unique position, but rather regarded Wheatleys as her true friends and benefactors. She did not become self-important because of her difference. Although she was invited to dine in homes of wealthy people, she learned to refuse a seat at the family table and to request that a sidetable be set up for her to dine apart.

Her best true friend was another black slave girl, named Obour Tanner, who probably came to America with Phillis. Obour lived in Newport, Rhode Island, and she and Phillis exchanged letters about once a year.

Phillis's first published poem was entitled *On Messrs Hussey and Coffin*. It was published in the *Newport Mercury* in Newport, Rhode Island, on December 21, 1767. It told the story of how two Wheatley family members were almost shipwrecked in a storm off Cape Cod.

On Messrs Hussey and Coffin

Did Fear and Danger so perplex your Mind,
As made you fearful of the Whistling Wind?
Was it not Boreas knit his angry Brow
Against you? or did Consideration bow?
To lend you Aid, did not his Winds combine?
To stop your passage with a churlish Line,
Did haughty Eolus with contempt look down
With Aspect windy, and a study'd Frown?
Regard them not; … the Great Supreme, the Wise
Intends for something hidden from our Eyes.
Suppose the groundless Gulph had snatch'd away
Hussey and Coffin to the raging Sea;
Where wou'd they go? Where wou'd be their Abode?

With the supreme and independent God,
Or made their Beds down in the Shades below,
Where neither Pleasure nor Content can flow?
To Heaven their Souls with eager Raptures soar,
Enjoy the Bliss of him they wou'd adore.
Had the soft gliding Streams of Grace been near,
Some favorite Hope their fainting hearts to cheer,
Doubtless the Fear of Danger far had fled;
No more repeated Victory crown their Heads.
    Had I the Tongue of a Seraphim, how would
    I exalt thy Praise; thy Name as Incense to
    the Heavens should fly, and the Remembrance
    of thy Goodness to the shoreless Ocean of
    Beautitude—Then should the Earth glow with
    seraphick Ardour.
Blest Soul, which sees the Day while Light doth shine,
To guide his Steps to trace the Mark Divine.

In 1768 Phillis wrote the poem describing her feelings about coming to America.

On Being Brought from Africa to America

'Twas mercy brought me from my *Pagan* land,
Taught my benighted soul to understand
That there's a God, that there's a *Saviour* too:
Once I redemption neither sought nor knew.
Some view our sable race with scornful eye,
"Their colour is a diabolic die."
    Remember, Christians, Negros black as Cain,
    May be refin'd and join th'angelic train.

A book of her poems was offered for publication in Boston in 1772, but all efforts failed, and the Wheatleys turned to an English publisher. The year before had brought many changes in the Wheatley household. Mary Wheatley married the Reverend John Lathrop, Phillis joined the Congregationalist Old South Meeting Church on August 18, and John Wheatley retired.

Nathaniel bought his father's business and part of the family home. When Nathaniel decided to take a business trip to England in 1773, the family urged him to take Phillis with him. She suffered from an asthmatic condition that was worsening, and they believed an ocean voyage would be strengthening. He agreed and they left Boston on May 8, 1773, on the London Packet and arrived in England on June 17 of that year.

Arrangements had been made previously with Archibald Bell, a bookseller in London, to publish a book of poems that Phillis had written, and the Countess of Huntington had kindly agreed to allow her own name to be used in the dedication, which would boost sales. The Countess was a devout Methodist, and she was willing to assist the young black girl in her artistic endeavors.

The Countess was also a friend of Susanna Wheatley. All were involved in the evangelical movement of the Reverend George Whitefield, known as the Great Awakening.

When the Reverend Whitefield died, Phillis wrote verses in his honor. Thomas Woolridge, a close friend of Whitefield, wrote a friend in England about Phillis.

His letter to the Earl of Dartmouth, dated November 24, 1772, described the young black poet as "a very Extraordinary female Slave, who had made some verses on our mutually dear deceased friend: I visited her mistress and found by conversing with the African she was no Imposter...."

Plans had been made for Phillis to visit the Countess while in England, but Phillis set sail back to Boston on September 13 when she learned Susanna Wheatley was seriously ill and John Wheatley had been badly injured in a fall and was unable to get out of bed without assistance. He freed Phillis from slavery shortly after her return, in December 1773.

Nathaniel Wheatley remained in England and married Mary Enderby there in November 1773. He never returned to Boston to live, but did bring his wife for a visit with relatives shortly after his mother's death early in 1774.

Phillis was greatly grieved by Mrs. Wheatley's death. She said she felt "like one forsaken by her parent in a desolate wilderness," and praised Mrs. Wheatley for her "uncommon tenderness for 13 years and unwearied diligence to instruct me in the principles of the true Religion."

Phillis wrote her friend Obour on October 30, 1773, that "my mistress has been very sick above 14 weeks and confined to her bed the whole time, but is, I hope, somewhat Better now." Mrs. Wheatley did live long enough to see a copy of the book of Phillis's poems, which was entitled *Poems on Various Subjects, Religious and Moral.* Phillis received her first copies in January 1774.

Although she was no longer owned by John Wheatley, Phillis elected to remain in his home and help with his care until he went to live in Chelsea during the British occupation of Boston. Then she went to stay with Mary and John Lathrop in Providence during the occupation.

Phillis wrote a poem about George Washington and sent it to him from Providence in October 1775, and Washington invited her to visit him in Cambridge in 1776, just before the British forces left Boston.

Her poem, entitled *To His Excellency, General Washington,* was as follows:

> Celestial choir! enthron'd in realms of light,
> Columbia's scenes of glorious toil I write.
> While freedom's cause her anxious breast alarms,
> She flashes dreadful in refulgent arms.
> See Mother Earth her offspring's fate bemoan,
> And nations gaze at scenes before unknown!
> See the bright beams of heaven's revolving light
> Involved in sorrows and the veil of night!
> The goddess comes, she moves divinely fair,
> Olive and laurel bind her golden hair:
> Wherever shines this native of the skies,
> Unnumber'd charms and recent graces rise.
> Muse! bow propitious while my pen relates

How pour her armies through a thousand gates:
As when Eolus heaven's fair face deforms,
Enwrapp'd in tempest and a night of storms;
Astonish'd ocean feels the wild uproar,
The refluent surges beat the sounding shore;
Or thick as leaves in Autumn's golden reign,
Such, and so many, moves the warrior's train.
In bright array they seek the work of war,
Where high unfurl'd the ensign waves in air.
Shall I to Washington their praise recite?
Enough thou know'st them in the fields of fight.
Thee, first in place and honours, ... we demand
The grace and glory of thy martial band.
Fam'd for thy valour, for thy virtues more,
Hear every tongue thy guardian aid implore!
One century scarce perform'd its destin'd round,
When Gallic powers Columbia's fury found.
And so may you, whoever dares disgrace
The land of freedom's heaven-defended race!
Fix'd are the eyes of nations on the scales,
For in their hopes Columbia's arm prevails.
Anon Britannia droops the pensive head,
While round increase the rising hills of dead.
Ah! cruel blindness to Columbia's state!
Lament thy thirst of boundless power too late.
Proceed, great chief, with virtue on thy side,
Thy ev'ry action let the goddess guide.
A crown, a mansion, and a throne that shine,
With gold unfading, *WASHINGTON!* be thine.

In her loneliness, Phillis married John Peters, a free black man, on April 1, 1778. She had not been able to get any more of her poems published in the turbulent days of British occupation. Peters was not highly respected by Phillis' friends. They described him as a shopkeeper who "wore a wig, carried a cane, and felt himself superior to all kinds of labor."

85

Peters deserted Phillis after a time when she had no more poems published. Their two children had died in infancy, and Phillis was pregnant for a third time when her husband left.

She found work as a maid in a boarding house, and a few months later, in 1784, three more of her poems were published. The last one, *Liberty and Peace* was considered the best of all. It was published under her married name.

Liberty and Peace

Lo! Freedom comes. Th' prescient Muse foretold,
All Eyes th' accomplish'd Prophecy behold:
Her Port described, *"She moves divinely fair,*
Olive and Laurel bind her golden Hair."
She, the bright Progeny of Heaven, descends,
And every Grace her sovereign Step attends;
For now kind Heaven, indulgent to our Prayer,
In smiling *Peace* resolves the Din of *War.*
Fix'd in *Columbia* her illustrious Line,
And bids in thee her future Councils shine.
To every Realm her Portals open'd wide,
Receives from each the full commercial Tide.
Each Art and Science now with rising Charms
Th' expanding Heart with Emulation warms.
E'en great *Britannia* sees with dread Surprize,
And from the dazzling Splendors turns her Eyes!
Britain, whose Navies swept th' *Atlantic* o'er,
And Thunder sent to every distant Shore:
E'en Thou, in Manners cruel as thou art,
The Sword resign'd, resume the friendly Part!
For *Galia's* Power espous'd *Columbia's* Cause,
And newborn *Rome* shall give *Britannia* Law,
Nor unremember'd in the grateful Strain,
Shall princely *Louis'* friendly Deeds remain.
The generous Prince th' impending Vengeance eyes,
Sees the fierce Wrong, and to the rescue flies.

Perish that Thirst of boundless Power, that drew
On *Albion's* Head, the Curse to Tyrants due.
But thou appeas'd submit to Heaven's decree,
That bids this Realm of Freedom rival thee!
Now sheathe the Sword that bade the Brave atone
With guiltless Blood for Madness not their own.
Sent from th' Enjoyment of their native Shore
Ill-fated—never to behold her more!
From every Kingdom on *Europa's* Coast
Throng'd various Troops, their Glory, Strength and
  Boast.
With heartfelt pity fair *Hibernia* saw
Columbia menac'd by the Tyrant's Law:
On hostile Fields fraternal Arms engage,
And mutual Deaths, all dealt with Mutual Rage;
The Muse's Ear hears mother Earth deplore
Her ample Surface smoak with kindred Gore:
The hostile Field destroys the social Ties,
And everlasting Slumber seals their Eyes.
Columbia mourns, the haughty Foes deride,
Her Treasures plunder'd, and her Towns destroy'd
Witness how *Charlestown's* curling Smoaks arise,
In sable Columns to the clouded Skies!
The ample Dome, high-wrought with curious Toil,
In one sad Hour the savage Troops despoil.
Descending *Peace* the Power of War confounds;
From every Tongue celestial *Peace* resounds;
As from the East th' illustrious King of Day,
With rising Radiance drives the Shades away,
So Freedom comes array'd with Charms divine,
And in her Train Commerce and Plenty shine.
Britannia owns her Independent Reign,
Hibernia, Scotia, and the Realms of Spain;
And great *Germania's* ample Coast admires
The generous Spirit that *Columbia* fires.
Auspicious Heaven shall fill with fav'ring Gales,

Where e'er *Columbia* spreads her swelling Sails:
To every Realm shall Peace her charms display,
And Heavenly *Freedom* spread her golden Ray.

Sadly, Phillis did not live to enjoy the publication of her works. She died at age 31 on December 5, 1784, in poverty and in childbirth. Her baby lived only a few hours longer. Their graves have been lost to time.

The *Independent Chronicle* newspaper ran the following notice of her death on December 8, 1784: "Last Lord's Day died Mrs. Phillis Peters (formerly Phillis Wheatley), aged 31, known to the world by her celebrated miscellaneous poems. Her funeral is to be this afternoon at four o'clock ... at West Boston, where her friends and acquaintances desired to attend."

Her husband later sold her books and manuscripts to pay his debts.

Bibliography

Barker-Benfield, G.J. and Clinton, Catherine. *Portraits of American Women.* New York: St. Martin's, 1991

DePauw, Linda Grant. *Founding Mothers.* Boston: Houghton-Mifflin, 1975.

Mason, Julian D., Jr. *The Poems of Phillis Wheatley.* Chapel Hill: University of N.C. Press, 1969.

Rawley, James A. *World of Phyllis Wheatley.* Boston: England Quarterly Magazine, 1977.

Williams, Selma R. *Demeter's Daughters: The Women Who Founded America, 1587–1787.* New York: Atheneum, 1976.

14

SUSANNA
HASWELL ROWSON
(1762–1824)

Susanna Rowson was both a playwright and an actress in a time when the theatre arts were considered to be socially unacceptable.

Susanna was born in 1762 in Portsmouth, England, to Lieutenant William Haswell of the British Army and his wife, the former Susannah Musgrove, the daughter of a customs commissioner. Mrs. Haswell died a few hours after her daughter was born and only had time to name her. Lieutenant Haswell had left England shortly before his daughter's birth to go to the colonies in America to fight Indians.

A kindly nurse took over the care of baby Susanna, which was fortunate, as Lieutenant Haswell was in no position to care for her himself.

Haswell remarried while he was in the colonies. His bride, Rachel Woodward, was older than he and a wealthy woman. He left the British Army and returned to England to claim his daughter in 1768.

In October of that year, Mr. Haswell, now employed by the British Revenue Service, left England with little Susanna and her nurse on a ship sailing to Boston.

They were on the sea in stormy turbulent weather until January 27, 1769. There was a shortage of food because of the length of the voyage, and on Christmas Day all the passengers were put on short food rations, under which each passenger received only a biscuit and a cup of water daily. The journey ended in a shipwreck on an island in Boston harbor.

Upon reaching Boston at last, Mr. Haswell took Susanna and her nurse to his home near Nantasket in Massachusetts. Mrs. Haswell's wealth allowed young Susanna to be well tutored. She became proficient in Greek and Latin and in the works of Homer, Virgil and Shakespeare.

A distinguished neighbor, James Otis, called Susanna "the little scholar" when he learned she read Shakespeare, Virgil and Homer at age 12. Some historians have believed Otis was her tutor.

In 1775, as the Revolutionary War began, Susanna's father requested permission from the authorities to return to England, but he was arrested by patriot forces in Massachusetts, his property was confiscated, and he and his family were placed under house arrest at Hingham for the next two years. They spent a third year in isolation at Abington. There Mr. Haswell developed a serious crippling illness.

In the spring of 1778, Mr. Haswell and Susanna were allowed to leave Massachusetts for Halifax, Nova Scotia, and from there they sailed to London.

In England Mr. Haswell petitioned the government for a pension to compensate him for his past services to the king, while Susanna found work as a governess, reportedly with Georgina, the Duchess of Devonshire.

Susanna worked as a governess from age 16 until she was 20, at which time she decided to write a book. She was supported in her efforts, both emotionally and financially, by the Duchess.

Susanna's book was entitled *Victoria*, and was supposedly based on events in the lives of people with whom Susanna was acquainted. The book is the story of a young woman, who falls in love with an immoral man and suffers as a result. Pathos was a desirable feature of the popular literature of the period, and the book sold fairly well. It was published in 1786 in England and was dedicated to the Duchess.

Susanna's father went to live near a military post in London, and while visiting him, Susanna met and married William Rowson, a trumpet player with the small military band there, the Royal Horse Guards. Rowson was also a hardware merchant.

Susanna soon discovered her own life to be an example of the plot of *Victoria*. Mr. Rowson was an alcoholic womanizer. Susanna stayed with him anyway, and wrote more novels, including one entitled *Charlotte Temple*.

Susanna's chief claim to fame lay in her authorship of *Charlotte Temple*, which was a sentimental story of a young English girl who was influenced by an English army officer to go with him to New York. There he later abandoned her, but was punished by deep remorse for his mistreatment of his conquest.

The book was published in London in 1791 and in Philadelphia in 1794. It has been reprinted in at least 200 editions and was the first best seller in America. She wrote a sequel called *Charlotte's Daughter, or The Three Orphans*, which was published in Boston in 1828 after her death. It did not enjoy the same success as her first book.

Charlotte Temple remained in print continuously from 1789 to 1906, more than 100 years. It has been reissued twice since World War II.

Since Susanna said the characters in her stories were based on the lives of real people, there was much speculation about the identity of the real Charlotte. The most widely accepted possibility was Charlotte Stanley, who was related to the Earl of Derby and who had a passionate love affair with John Montresor, an officer in the British Army.

As the years passed, William Rowson continued to drink and Susanna continued to forgive. When the hardware business he had started earlier failed in 1792, Susanna decided they should both go on the stage. William could play his trumpet and serve as a prompter, while Susanna would act in various roles in plays.

They began their careers on the stage in Edinburgh in the 1792–1793 season. Both of the Rowsons were then employed by Thomas Wignell to go with his "New Theatre" group to Philadelphia in America. It soon became evident that both William and

Susanna needed a lot of training to be effective entertainers, and as they crossed the Atlantic, Wignell took the opportunity to coach them.

Susanna was multi-talented and could sing and dance and play the guitar and harpsichord. She wrote lyrics for songs as well.

Susanna improved, as she had greatly desired a career as an actress, and she also wrote another novel on the voyage. By the time they reached Philadelphia, Susanna had a four-volume novel completed, entitled *Trials of the Human Heart*. It was published in 1795.

There was a severe epidemic of yellow fever in Philadelphia when they arrived, so the troupe went on to Annapolis in Maryland for their debut in Othello.

Susanna and William appeared with Wignell's group for the next two years, traveling between Philadelphia, Annapolis and Baltimore. Susanna was the first woman to play "Harlequin" in pantomime in American theatre.

Despite their busy performing schedule, Susanna continued to write her stories. She had turned her attention to putting her efforts in the form of plays, and she also wrote some lyrics for songs they used. When she combined both talents in the *Slaves of Algiers, or A Struggle for Freedom*, she became the originator of the early-nineteenth-century equivalent of Broadway musicals.

In the production of *Slaves of Algiers*, Susanna played the part of Olivia, a beautiful harem girl who rescues an American sailor from pirates on the Barbary Coast of Tripoli.

Audiences loved it, and Susanna enjoyed her greatest creative success in 1794 while it played.

William Rowson was getting drunk more often now, and in his carousing, he fathered an illegitimate son, also named William, whom he brought home to Susanna to rear.

Susanna loved the little boy and willingly cared for him. She and William were heartbroken when their son was lost at sea about 1812 while he was working as a seaman.

In 1796, Susanna and William went to live in Boston, leaving the Wignell troupe behind. Susanna wrote a play in Boston entitled *Americans in England*. When it was staged in the Federal Street

Theatre in Boston, both Susanna and William made their last stage appearances.

During her five-year career with the troupe, Susanna appeared in 126 different plays and played 129 different roles.

The year after Susanna retired from the stage, she started a finishing school for the young girls of Boston, which she named The Young Ladies Academy. Even though Boston citizens considered actresses in general to be women of uncertain morals, Susanna's school was a great success. She had a total of 60 students, 30 of whom boarded at the school.

Susanna never disguised her background, and in only three years, she had all the students she could manage in her school. She added piano lessons, languages, drama and dancing lessons to her curriculum, in addition to manners and social decorum.

Susanna turned her attention to writing textbooks for geography, science, drama, literature, and reading for use in her school, and for use in other schools as well.

The Slaves of Algiers continued to play for several years after Susanna and William had retired from the stage.

While appearing in the play in the Federal Street Theatre, Susanna met a musician named Gotlieb Graupner. She hired him to teach music in her school, and they collaborated in writing several songs, which were published. Mr. Graupner wrote the tunes for Susanna's lyrics.

Finally Susanna's health began to falter, and in 1822 she was forced to turn the operation of her school over to her niece Susan Johnston, and her adopted daughter, Fanny Mills. She continued to attend church regularly at Trinity Church, and served as president of the Boston Fatherless and Widows' Society for several years.

Susanna and William never had any children of their own but her boarding school students had filled a void in her life and she felt needed. By now she and William lived separately most of the time.

When Susanna died in Boston on March 24, 1824, she left many friends and numerous creative works behind.

She was buried in Mr. Graupner's family vault at Saint Matthew's Church in south Boston. When the church was torn down in 1866, her casket was transferred to Mount Hope Cemetery in Dorchester.

William outlived Susanna by several years, working as an inspector in the customs house in Boston. He married Hannah Bancroft after Susanna's death, but his last years are lost to history.

Bibliography

Neidle, Cecyle S. *America's Immigrant Women.* New York: Hippocrene Books, 1976.

Williams, Selma R. *Demeter's Daughters: The Women Who Founded America, 1587–1787.* New York: Atheneum, 1976.

15

SARAH
KEMBLE KNIGHT
(1666–1727)

Sarah Kemble Knight was a daring, brave woman who faced the perils of traveling on horseback, without a female companion, from Boston to New York by way of Rhode Island and New Haven, in 1704. In the journal she kept of her trip, she told of travel conditions for both women and men when they were forced to take long journeys, and the dangers they encountered.

Sarah was born in Boston on April 19, 1666, to Captain Thomas Kemble and his wife, the former Elizabeth Trerice, daughter of Nicholas Trerice, a shipmaster.

Captain Kemble was a wealthy merchant and a native of England. He had to travel extensively to obtain merchandise for his business.

Once, in 1656, when Captain Kemble returned from a trading voyage during which he had been away from home for three years, he gave his wife a kiss on their doorstep when he returned home. Since his return occurred on Sunday and he kissed his wife in public view, he was put in the public stocks for two hours as punishment.

The Kembles lived in a large house near New North Square in Boston, and little Sarah was educated by a tutor. Her journal entries indicate she received a broad education since she could compare laws in effect in Massachusetts at the time with those in effect in Connecticut.

Sarah married Richard Knight about 1684. Mr. Knight's father was also in trade, still living in London. Richard Knight had lived in both Boston and New York since he had come to America and he owned property in New York. He was employed as a brick mason and wood carver.

After their marriage, the Knights lived in the Kemble mansion on Moon Street in Boston, which Sarah had inherited from her father. Their daughter, Elizabeth Kemble, was born there on May 8, 1689, and was their only child.

Richard Knight died in 1702, and his will left all his property to his wife, including his real estate in New York. With a 16-year-old daughter to support, as well as herself, Sarah decided to go to New York and sell the property she had inherited. She kept a shop in their Boston home, but she knew she might need more money than she earned there.

Leaving Elizabeth safe at home, Sarah started on her trip on horseback on October 2, 1704, the same year the *Boston News Letter* began publication, the first newspaper published in any of the colonies.

Sarah planned to ride along with post riders as they made their deliveries of letters and packages, on their routes, which would give her protection from wild animals and/or Indian attacks as she rode. Her journey would take her through Rhode Island, Connecticut, and on to New York City.

When Sarah arrived at a wayside inn after the first long day of her trip, she wrote in her journal:

> My guide dismounted ... and showed the door, signing to me with his hand to go in, which I gladly did. But (I) had not gone many steps into the room ere I was interrogated by a young lady I understood afterwards was the eldest daughter of the family with ... words to this purpose, (viz) "Law for me—what in the world brings you here at this time-a-night? I never see a woman on the road so late in all my ... life. Who are you? Where are you going?"
> I'm scared out of my wits.... I stood aghast preparing no reply—when in come my guide. To him Madam turned, roaring

out: "Lawful heart, John, is it you? How de do? Where in the world are you going with this woman? Who is she?"

John made no answer but sat down in the corner. She turned again to me and fell anew into her silly questions without asking me to sit down.

I told her she treated me very rudely, and I did not think it my duty to answer her unmannerly questions. But to get rid of them, I told her I had come there to have the (Western) Post's company with me tomorrow on my journey...

I prayed Miss to show me where I must lodge. She conducted me to a parlour in a little back lean-to, which was almost filled with the bedstead, which was so high that I was forced to climb on a chair to get up to ye wretched bed ... on which having stretched my tired limbs and laid my head on a sad-colored (dingy) pillow, I began to think on the transactions of ye past day.

Tuesday, October ye third, 1704

About eight in the morning, I with the Post proceeded forward without observing any thing remarkable; and about two, afternoon, arrived at the Post's second stage, where the western Post met him and exchanged Letters. Here, having called for something to eat, ye woman brought in a Twisted thing like a cable, but something whiter; and laying it on the board, tugged for life to bring it to a capacity to spread; which having with great pains accomplished, she served in a dish of Pork and Cabbage, I suppose the remains of Dinner. The sauce was of a deep Purple, which I thought was boiled in her dye Kettle; the bread was Indian, and everything on the Table service Agreeable to these. I, being hungry, got a little down; but my stomach was soon cloyed, and what cabbage I swallowed served me for a cud the whole day after.

Having here discharged the Ordinary for self and Guide,(as I understood was the custom), about three (in the) afternoon went on with my Third Guide, who rode very hard; and having crossed Providence Ferry, we come to a River which they generally ride through. But I dare not venture; so the Post got a lad and a canoe to carry me t'other side, and herid (rode) through and led my horse.

The canoe was very small and shallow, so that when we were in, she seemed ready to take in water, which greatly terrified me, and caused me to be very circumspect, sitting with my hands fast on each side, my eyes steady, not daring so much as to lodge my tongue a hair's breadth more on one side of my mouth than t'other, nor so much as think on Lot's wife, for a wry thought would have overset our wherry; but(I) was soon put out of this pain, by feeling the canoe onshore, which I as soon almost saluted with my feet; and rewarding my sculler, again mounted and made the best of our way forwards....

We rode on very deliberately a few paces, when we entered a thicket of trees and shrubs, and I perceived by the horse's going, we were on the descent of a hill, which, as we come nearer the bottom, 'twas totally dark with the trees that surrounded it. But I knew by the going of the horse we had entered the water, which my Guide told me was the hazardous river he had told me of, and he, riding up close to my side, bid me not fear—we should be over immediately. I now rallied all the courage I was mistress of, knowing that I must either venture my fate of drowning, or be left like ye children in the wood. So, as the Post bid me, I gave reins to my nag; and sitting as steady as just before in the canoe, in a few minutes got safe to the other side, which he told me was the Narragansett country.

Sarah and the post rider were entering the boundaries of the Rhode Island colony. She continued in her journal:

Here we found great difficulty in traveling, the way being very narrow, and on each side the trees and bushes gave us very unpleasant welcomes with their branches and boughs, which we could not avoid, it being so exceedingly dark.

My Guide, as before so now, put on harder than I, with my weary bones, could follow; so left me and the way behind him. Now returned by distressed apprehensions of the place where I was—the dolesome woods, my company next to none, going I knew not whither, and encompassed with terrifying darkness; the least of which was enough to startle a more masculine courage....

By this time, poor Sarah must have wished she had never begun such an arduous journey, but she could not turn back now. She admitted that "my call was very questionable, which till then I had not so prudently as I ought considered."

Sarah Kemble Knight

However, she and her guide soon came up on another wayside inn where they could eat and rest. She wrote:

> Being come to Mr. Havens, I was very civilly received and courteously entertained, in a clean comfortable house; and the good woman was very active in helping off my riding clothes, and then asked what I would eat. I told her I had some chocolate, if she would prepare it; which with the help of some milk and a little clean brass kettle, she soon effected to my satisfaction.
>
> I then betook me to my apartment, which was a little room parted from the kitchen by a single board partition; where, after I had noted the occurrences of the past day, I went to bed, which though pretty hard, [was] yet neat and handsome.
>
> But I could get no sleep, because of the clamor of some of the town topers in the next room, who were entered into a strong debate concerning the signification of the name of their country, (viz) Narragansett…. I heartily fretted and wished them tongue-tied…. They kept calling for t'other gill, which while they were swallowing was some intermission, but presently like oil to fire increased the flame.

Sarah was tired and probably nervous about what other problems she might encounter as she continued on to New York. She tended to compose poetry to express her feelings, and she continued in her entry for that day:

> I set my candle on a chest by the bedside, and sitting up, fell to my old way of composing my resentments in the following manner:
>
> > I ask thy aid, O Potent Rum!
> > To charm these wrangling topers dumb.
> > Thou hast their giddy brains possessed
> > The man confounded with the beast.
> > And I, poor I, can get no rest.
> > Intoxicate them with thy fumes:
> > O still their tongues till morning comes!
>
> And I know not but my wishes took effect; for the dispute soon ended with t'other dram; and so Good night!…

A few days later when Sarah and her guide stopped at yet another inn, Sarah found she would be forced to share a room with some male travelers due to the lack of sleeping space. She was not happy with the arrangement, but she could do nothing otherwise. She had a low opinion of the accommodations, as she made clear in the pages of her journal:

> Arriving at my apartment, found it to be a little lean-to chamber furnished amongst other rubbish with a high bed and a low one, a long table, a bench and a bottomless chair. Little Miss went to scratch up my kennel, which rustled as if she'd been in the barn amongst the husks, and suppose such was the contents of the ticking. Nevertheless, being exceedingly weary, I laid my poor carcus (never more tired) and found my covering as scanty as my bed was hard.
> Anon I heard another rustling noise in ye room—called to know the matter—little Miss said she was making a bed for the men; who when they were in bed, complained their legs lay out of it by reason of its shortness....

Sarah added she arose about three o'clock in the morning and sat by the fire until daylight came.

When she reached Connecticut, Sarah found it more to her liking, and she stayed there for several weeks before continuing her journey. She wrote:

> (1704)
> They are governed by the same laws as we in Boston, or little differing, throughout this whole colony of Connecticut, and much the same way of church government, and many of them good, social people, and I hope religious too; but a little too much independent in their principles, and, as I have been told, were formerly in their zeal very rigid in their administrations toward such as their laws made offenders, even to a harmless kiss or innocent merriment among young people. Whipping being a frequent and counted as an easy punishment, about which as other crimes, the Judges were absolute in their sentences....

Sarah must have been acutely sensitive about being punished

for kissing in view of her father's placement in the stocks in Massachusetts for kissing his own wife on a Sunday.

She was fascinated by what she saw of Indians. She wrote, "there are everywhere in the towns as I passed, a number of Indians, the natives of the country, and are the most savage of all the savages of that kind that I had ever seen; little or no care taken, as I heard upon inquiry, to make them otherwise. They have in some places lands of their own, and governed by laws of their own making; they marry many wives and at pleasure put them away, and on the least dislike or fickle humor, on either side, saying 'stand away' to one another is a sufficient divorce. And indeed those uncomely 'Stand aways' are too much in vogue among the English in this indulgent colony, as their records plentifully prove, and that on very trivial matters, of which some have been told me, but are not proper to be related by a female pen...."

Sarah Knight reached New York in December 1704. She conducted her business there, but she also took time to record her impressions of that colony as well. Her journal says:

> They are generally of the Church of England and have a New England gentleman for their minister, and a very fine church set out with all customary requisites. There are also a Dutch and Divers Conventicles as they call them.... They are sociable to one another and courteous and civil to strangers and fare well in their houses.
>
> The English go very fashionable in their dress, but the Dutch, especially the middling sort, differ from our women in their habit, go loose, wear French muches which are like a cap and a headband in one, leaving their ears bare, which are set out with jewels of a large size and many in number. And their fingers hooped with rings, some with large stones in them of many colors, as were their pendants in their ears, which you should see very old women wear as well as young.

Sarah's travels and business dealings covered a period of five months. She got back to Boston on March 3, 1705. There she found "kind relations and friends flocking in to welcome me and hear the story of my transactions and travails...."

Sarah's daughter Elizabeth married a Colonel Livingston not long after her mother's return home, and the Livingstons went to live on the Colonel's large plantation near New London, Connecticut.

In the Autumn of 1705, Sarah started a school in her mansion in Boston. Author Hannah Mather Crocker wrote in 1818 in her *Observations of the Real Rights of Women*, that Sarah Knight was a "smart, witty, sensible women" and had "considerable influence" in Boston.

Sarah continued to operate her school until 1714. The next year she moved to Norwich, Connecticut, where she bought property and opened an inn of her own to care for weary travelers, no doubt drawing on her own experiences. The inn was located near Colonel Livingston's property.

Sarah apparently took an active part in the Norwich community and church. In 1717 she gave a silver communion cup to the church to use in their communion services.

In 1720, after her son-in-law's death, she moved to New London to live on some land she had bought there. She had another inn built in her new location and joined the Congregational North Parish Church.

Sarah died in New London in 1727, at age 61, and was buried there in the cemetery maintained by the town.

Bibliography

Chitwood, Oliver P., PhD. *A History of Colonial America*. New York and London: Harper and Brothers, 1931.

Williams, Selma R. *Demeter's Daughters: The Women Who Founded America, 1587–1787*. New York: Atheneum, 1976.

16

JANE
FRANKLIN MECOM
(1712–1794)

Jane Mecom was the beloved sister of Benjamin Franklin, the great patriot. Her life of poverty and hard work contrasted sharply with her brother's life of prestigious accomplishments in Europe as a representative of the new United States government in America.

She was born Jane Franklin on March 27, 1712, in Boston, to Josiah and Abiah Folger Franklin. She was one of ten children of her parents, and one of seventeen children of her father's, as he had been married previously.

Jane and Benjamin were children together in their parents' home along with two sisters, Lydia and Sarah. Other siblings had either died young or were married and living in homes of their own.

Jane received some formal education in her early years and was an avid reader, but her letters indicate spelling was not among her talents. Jane and Benjamin were always more compatible than either was with their other brothers or sisters, even though Benjamin was six years older than Jane, whom he called "Jenny."

Josiah Franklin had a soap and candle shop on the same lot as the family dwelling. There was a large blue metal ball mounted on a bracket above the shop to advertise its presence. Both candles and soap were needed in every household, so Josiah earned a good, although not excellent living. Family meals were frequently meat-with-vegetable stews for lunch, and cornmeal mush or bread and milk for breakfast and supper.

Josiah and his wife were Puritans, and they took their children with them to church regularly. Jane was a willing attendee at church services and a pious listener during their father's extended prayers twice each day, but Benjamin kept his eyes open and looked at maps adorning the walls of the dining area during family devotions.

Benjamin's lack of religious fervor was always a sore trial to Jane. She loved Benjamin more than anyone else in her life, and she worried about his future afterlife if he did not change his unorthodox beliefs and adopt the Christian faith.

When Jane was six years old, Benjamin was apprenticed to their older brother, James, to learn the printing trade. James Franklin was the owner and publisher of the *New England Courant* newspaper. Since the print shop was located in another area of Boston, Benjamin no longer lived with his parents but moved in with James.

The brothers got along fairly well until Benjamin reached the age of 17. At that time Benjamin tired of his brother's beatings and tongue-lashings and ran away to Philadelphia without any warning to anyone.

For weeks the Franklin family had no idea where Benjamin had gone, until another sister's husband, who was a sea captain, found out where he was. Jane, who had been distraught about his disappearance, felt great relief when she learned he was all right.

Benjamin got a job in Philadelphia as a printer, but about eight months later he returned home to Boston and asked his father to lend him money so he could open his own print shop.

Josiah Franklin felt he could not afford the investment, but when Benjamin returned to Philadelphia after his visit home, he went with his family's blessings and best wishes.

Without financial assistance from his father to open a shop of his own, Benjamin was forced to work as a store clerk to support himself. About three years later, Jane received the first of what would be many letters from Benjamin. He told her he had talked with Captain Isaac Freeman, a family friend, who gave him the latest news from Boston.

Benjamin wrote Jane,

> Dear Sister, I am highly pleased with the account Captain Free-
> man gives me of you. You know you were ever my peculiar
> favorite. I have been thinking what would be a suitable present
> for ... you to receive, as I hear you are grown a celebrated
> beauty.... I concluded to send you a spinning wheel, which I
> hope you will accept as a small token of my sincere love and
> affection.... I am, dear Jenny, your loving brother, Benjamin
> Franklin.

On July 27, 1727, Jane married Edward Mecom, a man with little money and less ambition. She was only 15 years old. Her parents
had to help the newlyweds by allowing them to live free in a house
they owned and normally rented. Edward worked as a market clerk,
but his earnings were not enough to support what soon became a
growing family.

By the time their seventh child was born, Jane was keeping
boarders to help support her family. Her boarders were poor, work-
ing-class people with humble jobs, and Jane did not make much
profit. She also had to assume much of the care of her parents after
her sister, Lydia, married Captain Robert Scott and left home.

During this period Jane began a regular correspondence with
Benjamin, still in Philadelphia, giving him news of the whole Franklin
family as well as her own. Four sisters and a brother had died since
he left, leaving only Jane, Lydia, John and Elizabeth in Boston.

In May 1743, Benjamin came to Boston to visit, and Jane was
delighted to see him. She was curious about his wife, Deborah, to
whom he had been married for the past 13 years, and their children.
Jane and Benjamin had not seen each other for nine years.

Benjamin learned that his brother John had moved into the
manufacturing of fine clear green soap which carried a crown imprint
as a trademark, an improved version of the soap that their father had
made years before in his shop. Jane told him her son Peter was an
apprentice to his Uncle John, to learn soapmaking.

Benjamin told her the soap was of fine quality and sold as well
in Philadelphia as it did in Boston.

When Jane's father died in January 1745, his will specified that two rooms in their house should be reserved for his wife's use during her lifetime, with the "lodgers to be in as now it is used." Jane and her family had been living in the house with her parents in recent months, and Jane was now pregnant with her ninth child.

Benjamin thanked Jane for her good care of their father during his last days, and told her to send her son Benny to New York to begin an apprenticeship there with a printer with whom Benjamin had made arrangements for the boy's training.

Benjamin also began sending Jane money to help pay living expenses. In 1752 their mother died, but Benjamin continued his interest in Jane's affairs.

After her mother's death, Jane found she and her husband were not financially able to pay the last year's rent on the boarding house, and Benjamin arranged for the Blue Ball house, which had formerly been used as their father's shop, to be sold.

About this same time, Jane's husband began a slow mental decline, and he was unable to work any more.

Jane and her husband moved to a larger house in Boston near an inn named the Orange Tree. By living there they hoped to attract some lodgers who either could not get a room at the popular Orange Tree or could not afford to pay the inn's prices.

Benny Mecom went to New York and worked briefly for the printer, as his Uncle Benjamin had suggested, but he did not stay long, and he had been drifting around from job to job, the most recent one being in Antigua. He could not get along well with his employers.

Peter Mecom had also left his uncle's shop and had gone to work for another soap maker after his Uncle John's death.

Jane worried about her two sons and their seeming inability to settle down, but she comforted herself with the thought that they were young and would find permanent jobs after a time.

Edward Mecom, Jane's husband, died September 11, 1765, after a long period of declining health. Jane continued to recruit boarders for her boarding house, even as she grieved for Edward.

Her sons were still wandering, looking for greater financial opportunities just over the horizon, and Jane knew she would have to be responsible for her own support.

In 1769 Jane was invited to come to Philadelphia and visit her sister-in-law Deborah, Benjamin's wife. Jane knew Benjamin had gone to Europe, but since she had never seen either his wife or any of their children, she decided to go.

Jane was not only curious about Benjamin's family; she also wanted to see their house and how they lived. She and Benjamin had been together so little as adults, she felt she hardly knew him in many ways.

Jane enjoyed her visit thoroughly. She was glad to be away from the bustling, noisy boarding house for a few weeks and to enjoy quieter surroundings. She fell while she was in Philadelphia and hurt her leg, but she insisted on completing her visit and returning home when she had planned.

Jane gained a real sense of Benjamin's prominence and importance in world affairs as she met his famous friends and read newspaper accounts of his diplomatic efforts in Europe. When Benjamin was criticized by friends and neighbors for his supposed part in the passage of the Stamp Act by the British Parliament, Jane defended him to one and all.

Benjamin was back home in Philadelphia when British troops invaded Boston on April 19, 1775. A family friend of the Franklin family, Catherine Ray Greene, wife of the governor of Rhode Island, invited Jane to take refuge with her and her family in Rhode Island.

Jane gladly joined the Greene household, and while there she made some crown soap like that her brother John had made in his shop years before. She gave Mrs. Greene some of the bars in appreciation for the family's kind treatment of her.

Jane spent almost four years in Rhode Island before she could return safely to her Boston home. Benjamin went back to Europe after the invasion and spent most of the four years there.

Benny and Peter Mecom were no longer employed anywhere. Both had developed mental problems, which appeared to be a genetic flaw in the Mecom family. Jane was discouraged about them and frightened about her own future.

When she finally got back to her Boston home, Jane found that much of her furniture and other possessions had been destroyed during the British occupation of the city. Benjamin arranged for Jane to live in a house that had belonged to one of their deceased sisters, which he had received as a legacy.

He wrote Jane, asking if she would send him some of the soap she had made, so he could give it as gifts to his European friends. She sent him two dozen cakes, which she admitted were "not of the very best possible, as you desired, owing to some unavoidable impediments, but sent it notwithstanding, as it will answer for your own use ... but would wish you not to make any presents of it."

Benjamin sent Jane a large package of clothing in return, some of which she used for herself. She wrote him: "the rest I sold and put the money to interest."

With her advancing age and weakening of her faculties, Jane's opportunities for earning money were dwindling.

Benjamin realized her financial resources were meager in the extreme, and he wrote to tell her he would send her 25 guineas, give her the rental income from a house he owned in Boston, and send her a fixed amount of money as long as she lived.

Jane's gratitude for his help was pathetic. She wrote: "How am I by my dear brother enabled to live at ease in my old age (after a life of care, labor and anxiety) without which I must have been miserable!"

Jane liked her new house better than the one the British soldiers had destroyed. She wrote Benjamin that her present home was cheerful and had more light. She wrote him about small changes she had made in the house, of which she was obviously proud.

As Jane grew older, she missed Benjamin more and more. His wife Deborah had died in 1774, and Jane conceived the idea that maybe she and Benjamin could set up a household together. Only a few of her children were still living.

Benjamin did not want to return to Boston to live. He knew Jane was not able to entertain his friends, as she was barely able to take care of herself. He wrote her:

Your project of taking a house for us to spend the remainder of our days in is a pleasing one, but it is a project of the heart rather than of the head. You forget, as I sometimes do, that we are grown old, and that before we can have furnished our house … we shall probably be called away from it to a home more lasting….

It was just as well Benjamin had not gone along with her plan, because by that fall her daughter and son-in-law, Jane and Peter Collas, had moved in with her. Captain Peter Collas had lost his job and had been unable to find another and they had nowhere else to go. Captain Collas was not a "go-getter."

Jenny Mecom, one of Jane's granddaughters, also came to live with Jane, and they shared a bedroom after the Collases had moved in.

In 1785 Jane spent the summer with Governor and Mrs. Greene in Rhode Island. While there, she got a letter from Benjamin asking if she would teach a young man named Jonathan Williams, Jr., how to make the crown soap. Along with the letter, he sent a bar of the soap she had made at the Greenes' during the Revolutionary War, to show her the quality he wanted kept in the line of soap.

Jane was pleased to realize Benjamin had kept the bar of soap as a reminder for at least the past five years.

By January 1, 1786, Jane had completed 60 pounds of the soap, with Mr. Williams' assistance, and she sent it to Benjamin in Philadelphia. She also sent him directions for making it.

Jane's recipe, which had been perfected by John Franklin before his death, involved setting leeches to catch lye water from wood ashes; leaving the lye water to cool and drawing the lye off the top when it would bear the weight of an egg; putting in clean, hard tallow and adding pure green bayberry wax to the mixture. Salt was to be added during the procedure to make the liquid soap clear; then the liquid was to be let cool, then cut when hardened and stamped with the crown design.

Benjamin and his daughter, Sally Bache, had difficulty in producing quality soap from Jane's recipe, however. He wrote Jane: "Sally … put three or four pounds of the crumbs (from their first batch) ... in a kettle with water and over a slow fire melted them together ... laded it out ... the size of ... cakes ... (but) in drying they are twisted and warped out of shape...."

Jane replied with the suggestion that they use 12 pounds of wax with 20 pounds of tallow. Plainly the quality of the soap mattered to Benjamin.

Jane refused payment for the soap she had sent him earlier, so he bought wood for her winter fires and sent her a barrel of flour. Captain Collas was unemployed again, and Benjamin knew she would be concerned about wood for winter.

On April 17, 1790, Benjamin died at the age of 84. All of Jane's hopes and dreams of them living together someday were ended. She would never be able to see him again.

Jane suffered with asthmatic attacks, and the grief she felt made her condition worse for a time. However, she knew she could live comfortably for the rest of her life thanks to Benjamin's generosity to her.

Jane lost interest in government affairs after Benjamin's death. She died in May 1795, at age 83.

Jane willed the house she and her family members had used for their home to her daughter, Jane Collas, to be used for her own home or rented, as she chose. To her beloved granddaughter Jenny, she left two rooms of furniture and all her personal effects.

Jenny married Captain Simeon Kinsman in 1801; sadly, Jane Collas survived her mother by only eight years.

Bibliography

Labaree, Leonard W. *Notable American Women, 1607–1950.* Cambridge: Belknap Press of Harvard University Press, 1971.

James, Edward T., Ed. *Notable American Women, 1607–1950.* Cambridge: Belknap Press of Harvard University Press, 1971.

17

SARAH WINSTON HENRY
(1710–1783)

Sarah Henry never made a speech in her life, but she helped train her son, Patrick, who became a loyal patriot in the American struggle for independence, and who helped rouse other citizens to fight for the cause.

Sarah was born Sarah Winston about 1710, to Isaac and Mary Dabney Winston. Sarah's ancestors on both sides of her family were established in the Virginia colony in the 1660s when the tide of immigration from England rose to high levels. They were not wealthy planters, but would be considered middle-class.

In 1726 Sarah married Colonel John Syme, who had recently come from Aberdeenshire in Scotland. Colonel Syme owned a large plantation in Hanover County in Virginia, comprising several hundred acres. It was called Studley Farm, and Colonel Syme and his workers spent most of their time cultivating tobacco.

The next year, a young kinsman of Colonel Syme's joined their household to help with the work. His name was John Henry. Young Henry needed to learn tobacco-farming methods to use on his own 400-acre tract lying in a more remote area of the county.

Since John Henry's land had never been cleared of its trees, he lived in the Syme household for about four years. He acted as farm manager for Colonel Syme when Syme was away from home on business.

In 1731, Colonel Syme died unexpectedly, leaving his 21-year-old widow and a young son, John Syme, Jr.

Sarah Syme was attractive enough in her appearance to attract the eye of the well-known connoisseur, Col. William Byrd, II.

Colonel Byrd spent a night at Studley Farm in 1732, when he found night approaching rapidly and no other sleeping quarters available. He described Sarah in his diary:

"A portly, handsome Dame ... much less reserved than most of her countrymen ... (which) became her well and set off her other agreeable qualities to good advantage."

Several months later, Sarah married John Henry, and they lived at Studley Farm for almost 20 years, during which time their children were born. John Syme, Jr., lived with them. When he reached maturity, he would own the Studley Farm as an inheritance from his father.

John Henry's family were literate and more literary than wealthy. As a cousin, David Henry, wrote in his London magazine, *The Country Gentleman*, the family was "more respected for their good sense and superior education than for their riches."

Men who bore the Henry last name became clerics and officials in both the Anglican Church and the Church of Scotland, which was Presbyterian.

Sarah and John Henry's first child was William, who became interested in Indian lore and tribal life at an early age and spent weeks at a time with the Indians in their camp, where he and they hunted and fished.

The Henrys' second child, born May 29, 1736, was christened Patrick, named in honor of his father's older brother. The older Patrick Henry was rector of the nearby Saint Paul's Anglican Church.

Sarah and John then had a total of nine daughters born of their marriage, making a sizable family. The sons attended a private school near their home, but the girls had to be content to learn housewives' skills and childrearing. They found it difficult to converse with strangers who visited in their home.

In England in the 1740s, an Anglican clergyman named George Whitefield began a religious revival which was aimed at reforming the Church from within. He brought the revival to the New World, and the Great Awakening, as the revival effort was called, soon spread throughout the colonies. In 1745 Mr. Whitefield came to the Hanover County area, and asked Sarah's brother-in-law, Patrick, for permission to use his church for religious services.

The Reverend Henry had been reluctant to grant permission to Whitefield, as he did not approve of Whitefield's passionate and tumultuous religious services. Henry preferred the more sedate type of worship. However, the Reverend Whitefield was at that time in good standing in the Anglican Church, so the Reverend Henry granted him permission to use the church.

Sarah Henry was thrilled to have an opportunity to hear Whitefield preach the Gospel. She took most of her children with her to the services he conducted.

Sarah enjoyed hearing well-prepared sermons, even though her personal views were closer to those of a dissenter. Her father, also a dissenter, was fined by the General Court about this time for allowing "unlicensed" meetings to be held in his home by traveling preachers.

Two years later, in 1747, a young preacher named Samuel Davies was licensed in Williamsburg to preach for Presbyterians in Hanover County. The Reverend Henry protested vehemently that the Reverend Davies should not have been allowed to come in and upset the Saint Paul's parish members with his ideas. To Henry's chagrin, his own sister-in-law Sarah preferred to attend the services conducted by the Reverend Davies.

Young Patrick Henry accompanied his mother, also with enthusiasm, to hear the Reverend Davies. Patrick had quit going to school at age 10 because he resented the severe beatings inflicted on the schoolboys by their instructors, and he had little interest in the subjects taught.

Reverend Davies was well-educated, and he brought topics to Patrick's attention which inspired the boy to pursue further study. Patrick considered the Reverend Davies to be the greatest speaker he had ever heard. He would use Mr. Davies' speaking arts later in his own life, when he rallied patriots to the cause of freedom.

Sarah wanted to be sure her son really listened to the sermons.

As they rode home in their horse-drawn gig, she would ask Patrick to tell her what text the preacher had used, and what he said about it. One of Patrick's relatives later observed that "she could have done her son no greater service." Patrick learned to organize his thoughts, to think deeply about the subject at hand, and to speak clearly.

Patrick's father was also well-educated, having attended King's College in Scotland for four years, studying Latin, Greek, ancient and modern history, geography, mathematics, philosophy and even theology. With this background, Mr. Henry decided to open a school for his own sons and the neighborhood children.

Sarah agreed that their sons needed more education, and she was relieved by her husband's decision. In addition, the fees paid by the parents of the other children would be useful in paying bills owed by the Henry family.

Later, young Patrick tried his hand at operating a retail store with his brother William, but the enterprise failed, in part because William still preferred to travel with the Indians.

Meanwhile, Sarah's firstborn son, John Syme, reached maturity and took over the Studley Farm, which he turned into a horse farm. Sarah and John Henry moved, with their own children, to a small plantation Henry had bought called Mount Brilliant in the Piedmont area of Virginia.

Patrick married a neighbor, Sarah Shelton, at age 18, and the newlyweds went to live as tenants on a farm owned by her father. When their house burned, they went to live in Shelton's Tavern, where Patrick assisted his father-in-law from time to time in serving customers of the tavern.

Shelton's Tavern was patronized by local lawyers, judges and other court officials. Current litigation was discussed freely in Patrick's hearing. Again, he listened closely to the conversations and became so interested that he began studying law on his own. A few years later he obtained his law license.

Another factor which may have influenced Patrick's decision to study law was his father's appointment, some years earlier, to serve as a Justice of the Peace. He was appointed by the General Assembly.

Patrick's law practice prospered, and within a few years he was able to buy a small plantation near that of his aging parents, who still lived at Mount Brilliant.

Sarah and John Henry were proud of Patrick and his accomplishments. Their oldest son, William, finally settled down to work and became a successful middle-class planter in his later years.

John Henry died in 1775, before Patrick had been chosen to be a delegate to the first Continental Congress in Philadelphia. It was in 1775, at the Provincial Convention, that Patrick made the famous speech in which he said: "I know not what course others may take, but as for me, give me liberty or give me death!" Sarah went to live with one of her daughters, Jane Meredith, after John Henry's death. Samuel Meredith, Jane's husband, was fond of Sarah and wrote Patrick after her death in 1783:

> She has been in my family upward of 11 years, and from the beginning to the end of that time, it most evidently appeared to me that it was one continued scene of piety and devotion, guided by such a share of good sense as rendered her amiable and agreeable to all who were so happy as to be acquainted with her.

Sarah would have been greatly pleased by his words.

Bibliography

Billings, Warren M., Selby, John E., and Tate, Thad W. *Colonial Virginia: A History*. Millwood, N.Y.: KTO Press, 1986.

Bowen, Catherine Drinker. *Miracle at Philadelphia*. Boston, New York and London: Little, Brown, 1986.

18

PENELOPE
PAGETT BARKER
(1728–1787)

Penelope Pagett seemed an unlikely candidate for a reformer role in the American colonies, and particularly unlikely to defy royal decrees about taxes in the colonies. Penelope was a socialite, and often such people prefer to maintain the status quo.

She was born in Chowan County in the North Carolina colony on June 17, 1728, to Doctor Samuel and Elizabeth Blount Pagett. She was the second of three daughters in the family, and she developed into a beautiful, charming woman.

Penelope lived the easy social life of a young woman who had friends among the wealthier and more influential people in her hometown of Edenton, North Carolina. There were elaborate balls and parties, which included dancing; also lesser "get-togethers" such as teas and church suppers.

Her father died when Penelope was 19, and the management of his estate was assumed by John Hodgson, husband of Penelope's sister Elizabeth. Hodgson was a lawyer.

A short time later, Elizabeth Hodgson also died, leaving two young sons and a little daughter. Penelope did not question her duty, which she believed included the care of the three orphaned Hodgson children.

The children loved their Aunt Penelope, and before many months had passed, John Hodgson asked Penelope to marry him.

Penelope had become fond of her brother-in-law through her close association with him and his family, and they were married.

They had two sons of their own as time passed. Their names were Samuel and Thomas. The year of 1747 was both sad and happy for Penelope. Her husband died, but her son Thomas was born.

As more time went by, Penelope attracted the attention of John Craven, a bachelor, and he asked her to marry him. Apparently, he had no objections to acquiring a ready-made family of five children. He too lived only a few years after their marriage, and at his death Penelope found he had left all of his property to her and the children.

Penelope's next husband was Thomas Barker, also an attorney. Barker had come from Massachusetts to Bertie County in North Carolina in 1735, at age 22. He had been married, but his wife had died, leaving a young daughter named Betsey.

Penelope and Thomas had three children of their own, but none lived to their first birthday. With all the assorted feverish illnesses prevalent along the lowland coastal regions, the other children also had short life spans. Penelope's son, Thomas, died at age 25 and her stepson John Hodgson in 1774.

Death was an ever-present enemy in the early days of the United States, but Penelope stayed busy at home and active in society to help her cope with her losses and further her husband's law and political career.

Mr. Barker was named Treasurer of the North Carolina Province and Assembly Clerk in October 1774. He and Penelope were an attractive, dynamic couple in Edenton, according to contemporary accounts, and they had many friends. They rode in a beautiful white coach decorated with the Barker coat of arms and pulled by a team of splendid horses.

Tea parties were much in vogue during this period of Edenton history, but they were not like the tea parties of today. These tea parties were more like today's cocktail parties, with both men and women as guests. They served as an opportunity for women to exchange gossip, while the men indulged in political discussions. The women's topics must have included politics at times, for future events would prove they were well-informed.

When colonists from Massachusetts to Georgia protested onerous taxes imposed on them by the English government, the ladies
in Edenton decided to take a stand on the subject of the recent impo-
sition of a tax on tea from England.

Penelope and a friend, Mrs. Elizabeth King, arranged a tea party
for 48 women guests on October 25, 1774, instead of serving tea,
they asked their friends to sign a pledge that they would no longer
serve English tea at their tables. The pledge declared:

> We, the ladyes of Edenton, do hereby solemnly engage not to
> conform to ye pernicious Custom of Drinking Tea, or that we,
> the aforesaid Ladyes, will not promote ye wear of any manufac-
> ture from England, until such time that all Acts which tend to
> enslave this our Native Country shall be repealed.

Most all of the guests signed, including Penelope. The women
did not throw tea in the ocean as the men had at Boston, but their
action was noted by the English authorities.

Men were largely amused by the tea party. Arthur Iredell,
brother of the James Iredell who would later be a member of the
first Supreme Court in the United States, wrote from his home in
England to his brother in Edenton:

> Is there a female Congress in Edenton too? I hope not....
> Ladies ... have ever since the Amazonian Era, been esteemed
> the most formidable Enemies ... each wound they give is mor-
> tal.... The more we strive to conquer them, the more (we) are
> conquered.

The Edenton Tea Party was the earliest recorded political activity by a group of women in any of the original 13 colonies.

A few weeks after the tea party, Mr. Barker sailed for England
on colony business. He was forced to remain there for several months
because of the beginning of the Revolutionary War, leaving Penelope alone in their Edenton home, except for their servants.

One day a servant rushed into the house to tell Penelope that
British soldiers were stealing the Barkers' horses from the barn.

Penelope did not hesitate. She reached for a sword mounted on a wall and rushed outside. An officer of the British Army sat astride one of the Barker horses, and Penelope severed the reins he was holding with a quick slash of the sword she held in her hand.

She demanded that the soldiers put the horses back in the stables and leave at once, as she cut the reins on the other horses.

The British soldiers were so impressed by her quick, decisive actions and bravery that they left without taking even one horse.

Penelope died some time after her husband's death in 1787, but the date is uncertain. A plaque honoring her leadership at the tea party in North Carolina was dedicated 1908 by the North Carolina Daughters of the American Revolution, and placed in the Capitol Building in Raleigh.

Bibliography

Lefler, Hugh T. and Powell, William S. *Colonial North Carolina: A History.* Millwood, N.Y.: KTO Press, 1981.

Rogers, Lou. *Tar Heel Women.* Raleigh, N.C.: Warren, 1949.

Williams, Selma R. *Dementer's Daughers: The Women Who Founded America, 1587–1787.* New York: Atheneum, 1976.

19

MERCY OTIS WARREN
(1728–1814)

Mercy Warren has been called by some historians "The First Lady of the Revolution," and whether or not she deserved the title, it is a fact that Mercy did help shape policies and ideas for a government for the new United States following the Revolutionary War.

Mercy was born in Barnstable, Massachusetts, on September 25, 1728, to Colonel James and Mary Allyne Otis. She was the first girl born to her parents, who already had two sons, James and Joseph.

A sister of Colonel Otis, who was also named Mercy, welcomed the arrival of her little namesake. The older Mercy was the wife of the Reverend Jonathan Russell, local pastor of the Barnstable Church, which was attended by both families.

As little Mercy and her brothers grew, the Reverend Russell assumed responsibility for their education. He was a graduate of Yale College and well educated, but since the saving of souls was not highly profitable in a monetary sense, he welcomed the fees paid by the parents of his students, as well as the farm produce he received as a bonus.

Young James Otis was an eager scholar and a source of pride to his teacher and the Otis family. Joseph Otis, his brother, was energetic and restless. He sought wider horizons than the classroom. He would become a brigadier general and serve as a member of the legislature in his later years, but when he left his studies and married while still in his teens, the Otis family despaired of his future success.

How does anyone explain Mercy's broad education, particularly regarding government affairs and political ideas and knowledge? In that day and age, if a woman could read and write legibly she was considered sufficiently educated. For some unknown reason, Mercy was allowed to study along with her studious brother, James, and she proved to be as apt at learning as he. She did not study Latin or Greek, however, although James studied both.

Mercy devoured with her eager mind the classical literature to which she was exposed, and found the study of history equally fascinating.

Even as Mercy was receiving what was considered excessive education for a woman, she also learned all the skills she would need as a housewife. She was an accomplished embroiderer, and wore a lavishly embroidered satin dress she had made for her trousseau.

Mercy learned to express her thoughts in writing by watching the Reverend Russell compose his sermons. Other girls of her era were taught chiefly to write personal letters, which expressed flowery sentiments, but Mercy wrote factually, thoughtfully and to the point.

When James Otis was fully prepared, he entered Harvard College. No such opportunity was offered to Mercy, and she missed having her brother in the classroom with her, if she had many more classes. The Reverend Russell allowed her to continue using his library and advised her about desirable books to read to further her knowledge.

Mercy had never been outside of Barnstable before James graduated from Harvard. She was suitably dressed in a silk dress to attend his graduation ceremony, and she went with her parents willingly. She found the boat ride to Boston and subsequent carriage ride to Cambridge to be thrilling beyond all her expectations, and she observed every detail of the oratory, sermons and feast, which were all parts of the graduation.

It was while she was in Cambridge that Mercy met James Warren for the first time. Warren was a sandy-haired, witty and handsome young man from Plymouth, who was a close friend of James Otis.

Mercy was immediately attracted to Warren, but it would be four years before they met again.

James Otis came home after graduation to study for his Master of Arts degree. Life had been on the dull side for Mercy while James was gone, but now she resumed her own studies vigorously.

After James received his degree, he went to Boston to study law with the attorney general of the province. He continued to do well in his law studies, but he developed an odd habit of walking away unexpectedly from legal meetings, parties, and other social gatherings. He offered no explanations or apologies for his conduct.

James decided to set up a law practice in Plymouth when he had qualified as a lawyer. There he renewed his friendship with James Warren, who was now a Plymouth merchant and farmer. When James went home to visit his family back in Barnstable, Warren went with him.

After they met again, Mercy and James Warren began a courtship which would lead to their marriage in November 1754.

The newlyweds went to live on the Warren farm on the banks of the Eel River near Plymouth. With the heavy Massachusetts winter snows, weeks of isolated living and farm chores to be done daily, Mercy found living at the Eel River farm to be not much different from her old life in Barnstable.

Six months later, James Otis also married. His bride was Ruth Cunningham, daughter of one of Boston's wealthiest merchants. Otis found it hard to adjust to married life, and he continued to spend much of his free time with the teachers of Boston Latin School.

After three years of living at the Warren farm, James and Mercy bought a large town residence in Plymouth. They made this purchase their real home, and used the house on the Eel River farm for a country vacation home. James Warren also continued to farm the land, however.

He and Mercy had not started their family until they moved to Plymouth. From that time, their five sons were born at roughly two-year intervals—James in 1757, Winslow in 1759, Charles in 1762, Henry in 1764, and George in 1766. The Warrens never had a daughter, and, rare for the time, had no children who died in infancy.

Meanwhile, James Otis had developed a prosperous law practice in Boston. He became King's Advocate for the colony's courts, and received a handsome salary. He and his wife, with their three children, should have been able to enjoy some of life's finer moments, but there was serious conflict in their home.

James Otis had studied statesmanship and political thinkers' writings since childhood, as had Mercy. James, Mercy and James Warren, along with other colonial leaders, were beginning to believe the time had come for the New World colonies to break free of English rule and become self-governing.

Ruth Otis, however, was an adamant Tory and supported English control of their lives. She did not understand even half of the arguments James presented to her about the desirability of making the colonies independent of the Crown, and she made no effort to hide her displeasure with James and his associates.

As tensions mounted between the governments of England and those of the colonies, James Otis became more excitable and talkative, as his good friend, John Adams, wrote:

> I'm sorry for James Otis. He has often told me that his wife was a high Tory and read him the most unmerciful curtain lectures. It's my guess that friction at home as much as anything has been the cause of the irritability that has broken his fine mind and got him into trouble.... Otis talks all.... [H]e grows the most talkative man alive; no other gentleman in company can find a space to put in a word....

When James Otis inserted a notice in the *Boston Gazette* stating that revenue officers appointed by the English government were falsely accusing him of inciting a rebellion against the Crown, Mercy and his friends feared for his safety.

Indeed, the rash action by James Otis provoked a serious attack by the officers, who ambushed James one night and beat him unmercifully. They injured his head, and from that time on James Otis was mentally disabled. He could no longer work at all and had to have a caretaker.

Mercy was horrified that her beloved brother had been so treated by representatives of the English government, and she and her husband began holding meetings of rebellion-minded colonists in their home. She felt if James could no longer carry the torch for freedom in his present state of diminished capability, it was her duty to do so.

James Warren supported fully the aims of his wife, and he invited his fellow patriots to meet in their home so Mercy could enter into the discussions they held. One of their first practical organizational methods was devised in Mercy's parlor—that of forming committees for correspondence.

The patriots in all the colonies needed a method by which they could learn of plans and events of other patriots, and letters written by committees would furnish the link they needed. The committees also assumed some control of government functions when the British were being driven out of the colonies.

Mercy had been writing poetry since she was a schoolgirl, and with these new developments in the colonies, she turned her attention to writing plays. One major handicap she faced in her efforts was that Mercy had never seen a play performed. In Massachusetts, theaters were forbidden entirely by the blue laws, and Mercy had never been in another colony.

Shakespeare and Molière wrote plays that Mercy had always enjoyed reading, so she decided to write plays for people to read. She used the vehicle of stage dramas to satirize the political scene.

She was successful from the beginning, and *The Adulateur* was published in a newspaper first in serial form and later in a pamphlet in 1773. Her second play, *The Defeat*, also appeared first in a newspaper in two installments the same year.

The characters in the two plays were thinly disguised local officials then in power by the edict of the British government. The leading target of Mercy's pen was the colonial governor, Thomas Hutchinson, who had been instrumental in the sad fate befalling James Otis.

The plays were read with glee by colonists of all classes, and, despite her busy life as a wife and the mother of five active young boys, Mercy somehow found time to continue with her writing.

Mercy's proof that her writing was an effective instrument for change came when Governor Hutchinson was called to England to explain to the king how he had so underestimated the revolutionary mood in Massachusetts. Hutchinson was removed from office, and he remained in England against his will for the rest of his life.

In 1774 British General Thomas Gage took control of Boston, and one of his first projects included the arrests of John Adams, Samuel Adams, John Hancock and other patriots such as James Warren. When Gage tried to locate the men, however, they were not to be found. Most were in Philadelphia at the Continental Congress sessions, where some of them were serving as delegates.

Mercy and James Warren were in Rhode Island visiting the governor, with whom James had business dealings. They made the trip on horseback, and Mercy could not have taken many clothes with her.

Mercy had recently published her third play, *The Group*, also a political satire. It appeared in pamphlet form, and was published by a Boston publisher on April 3, 1775. While General Gage occupied Boston, John Adams asked James Warren to send a copy of the play to him in Philadelphia, where it achieved widespread success with readers in both New York and Philadelphia.

John Adams was openly enthusiastic about Mercy's writings, and he told her she should write the history of the struggles of the emerging nation of the United States.

However, Mercy had begun wondering if her success in writing political satire was unfeminine. She wrote to John Adams's wife, Abigail, to ask her opinion. Abigail and Mercy were friends of several years' standing, and Mercy felt she would be honest.

Abigail admired everything about Mercy, from her abilities as an author to her methods of child rearing, and she assured Mercy that she had nothing to fear about her femininity.

When the Revolutionary War began in earnest, James Warren was named Major General of the Massachusetts militia, and his actual job was to be Paymaster General of the whole army under the command of General George Washington. Mercy visited James frequently, wherever his company was in camp, and she met Martha Washington at Valley Forge where Martha had gone to spend the winter with her husband George, now General Washington. Despite the evidence of war all around them, the couples dined together, and the women managed to provide some small entertainments for the other officers and their wives who happened to be in camp.

As the war continued, Mercy visited her friend Abigail Adams whenever she could. Abigail was efficiently managing the Adams farm while her husband, John, was serving in the Continental Congress. Mercy admired Abigail for her farming abilities, which Mercy lacked.

Mercy's son Winslow was old enough to be a soldier, but he was supposedly needed at home to help his mother do farm work. However, he was as lacking in agricultural skills as she, and he was becoming restless.

In the Army, James Warren often had to use his own money to buy supplies for the troops. He did not have a fortune to start with, and he and other patriots dipped deep into whatever reserves they had in order to finance the war effort.

Their efforts to supply the troops caused their families to suffer monetary difficulties. Sam Adams's wife, Betsy, took in sewing to support their family while Sam was at the Continental Congress.

When General Gage finally left Boston and moved southward, Mercy had new worries about her son, James, Jr., who had joined the Navy. She feared her husband would follow the Army to the south, and she begged him not to leave the area when the Army moved. She felt she was reaching the limit of her endurance.

Mercy had no need to worry. Her husband was busily organizing privateer ships in Boston harbor to enlarge the Continental Navy. This new group would be assigned to sink incoming British supply ships before they could get into port. His headquarters would be in Boston for the indefinite future.

Just as Massachusetts residents were returning home after the British invasion, a smallpox epidemic began in the Boston–Plymouth area. Mercy and Abigail took their children to Boston to be inoculated against the disease. While they were in Boston, the Declaration of Independence was formally read there—wonderful news indeed for the patriots!

James Warren wrote John Adams, who was still in Philadelphia: "Your Declaration of Independence came on Saturday and diffused a general joy. Everyone of us feels more important than ever. We now congratulate each other as Freemen."

When British General John Burgoyne wrote a play entitled *The Blockade of Boston*, in which colonial soldiers and their military efforts were ridiculed, Mercy replied in kind. She wrote *The Blockheads; or The Affrighted Officers: A Farce: Boston.*

In her play, Mercy used women characters for the first time, and also the language in this latest play was frank and coarse. Mercy was not a stranger to bawdy language: her brother, James Otis, had greatly enjoyed hearing and telling off-color jokes before his illness.

As the Revolutionary War dragged on, Mercy became discouraged. She wrote nothing for the next three years. Her father was old and sick, and James Otis had begun wandering away from his father's home as his own confusion deepened. Her own husband and oldest son were directly involved in the war, Winslow had left home and was living in Boston, and Charles had begun his studies at Harvard.

In 1778 Mercy began having health problems of her own, especially with her eyes. She was particularly distressed about Winslow's absence from home and apparently feared he might get into some sort of trouble. She wrote him to be wary of "associates who make a show of distinction without having any real worth."

Mercy turned back to writing for self-comfort, and she wrote *The Motley Assembly*, a blast at snobbery among ladies in American society. It was a comedy with a bite in it about turncoats and Tory-born citizens, as well as those patriots who still cherished the social class system of old England.

Winslow Warren then decided he would seek fame and fortune in Europe. He left Boston on May 17, 1780, destined for Holland where he planned to buy items for import and resale in Boston. The ship on which he sailed was captured by the British, and Winslow spent an entire summer in prison in Newfoundland, after which he was taken on to London by his captors.

Winslow enjoyed being in London, but Mercy worried about him. Her fears were realized when Winslow was again detained by

British officials for a time because he was suspected of being a spy, which he was not.

Winslow was interviewed three times by Lord Hillsborough, Secretary for the Colonies, who urged Winslow to "persuade his father and friends to submit to the best of Kings." Winslow was then allowed to go on to Holland.

James Warren, Jr., lost one of his legs while on duty with the Navy, and Charles Warren returned home from Harvard because he had developed tuberculosis.

Winslow wandered around in Europe for a time, then traveled back and forth to Massachusetts, piling up debts as he went. Hoping an ocean voyage would improve his own health, Charles Warren left to visit Winslow, who was then in Portugal. Unfortunately, Charles was in worse condition than he realized, and he died before seeing Winslow.

Another of Mercy's sons, Henry, had planned to enter a business venture with Charles. After Charles died, Henry decided to go ahead with his plans and left for Plymouth.

James Otis, Mercy's beloved brother, was killed by a lightning bolt during a thunder storm in May 1783. Mercy's troubles multiplied every year, but she continued to write her plays.

In *The Ladies of Castile*, Mercy described her heroine as one who defied tyranny and used church treasury funds to pay an army of citizens. In *The Sack of Rome*, the actual course of history was brought to life by the play's characters. Each play involved about a year's work by Mercy.

Mercy and James moved back to Plymouth and the Eel River farm after the Revolutionary War ended, and about the same time the Constitution was adopted. There were parts of the Constitution the Warrens did not like; however, after the Bill of Rights was added, they felt it was adequate.

In 1791 Winslow Warren was put in debtors' prison in Massachusetts. Apparently his parents could not afford to help him any more, and they had to endure the pain of seeing him punished.

When he was released from prison a few months later, Winslow joined the new Army of the United States. He was commissioned as a Second Lieutenant, and it appeared his fortune had changed for the better.

Sadly, however, he was killed a few weeks later during a surprise Indian attack on the Army camp while he was sleeping.

Mercy was overcome by grief when Winslow died. She had always considered him the brightest and best of her children. She wrote her youngest son, George, now living in Maine:

> Oh, how I do regret that we did not all unite to prevent, if possible, our dear Winslow engaging in the late fatal expedition. For myself I have never had a moment's quiet since I saw the direction that announced his appointment. ...

George also died young, at age 34, during a bitterly cold Maine winter in 1799. Neither of his parents could go to him, and when his brother Henry finally got to George's home in March, George had been buried, making three of the Warren sons who had died untimely deaths.

Mercy turned again to her writing—this time a historical account of the Revolutionary War. James Warren, Jr., had been teaching school in Hingham, and he moved back to Plymouth. Mercy was delighted to have him near, especially as he helped her with her secretarial needs. Her eyesight was failing badly now.

A few months later, James, Jr., received an appointment as Postmaster of Plymouth, which further helped with family finances.

When Mercy's *History of the Rise, Progress and Termination of the American Revolution* was completed, it was published in three volumes. Since various male authors wrote books about the same era, Mercy's book did not reach the number of readers for which she had hoped. A second edition was not published.

When their old friend John Adams was elected the second President of the United States, Mercy wrote a letter of congratulations to Abigail, but James Warren ignored his old friend's honor. Both he and Mercy disliked Adams' Federalist beliefs and policies.

John Adams was hurt by James Warren's hostility, but he did not protest it. However, when he read Mercy's *History*, he exploded in anger. Among other pointed remarks in her book, she said of John Adams and his administration:

> Mr. Adams was undoubtedly a statesman of penetration and ability; but his prejudices and his passions were sometimes too strong for his sagacity and judgment ... it was viewed as a kind of political phenomenon when (it was) discovered that Mr. Adams' former opinions were beclouded by a partiality for monarchy.... After Mr. Adams' return from England he was implicated by a large portion of his countrymen as having relinquished the republican system, and forgotten the principles of the American Revolution, which he had advocated for near 20 years....

Adams dashed off a letter to Mercy, in which he forcefully expressed his concern for his reputation in history after the criticisms she had written of him. He had never expected her to air their differences in political views in public.

James Warren, Mercy's husband, was now an invalid and he stayed out of their quarrel. He died soon after on November 28, 1808.

John Adams refused to write a letter of condolence to Mercy about her loss. Abigail Adams had been as upset as John with Mercy, but she began to relent in her antagonism toward her after Elbridge Gerry, a mutual friend, urged her to write Mercy an answer to the letter Mercy had written to President Adams.

Abigail took his advice, and in August 1812, she drove over to Plymouth to visit with Mercy. Later they exchanged brooches in which each women had set a lock of her own hair, a widespread custom of the time.

Henry Warren was the only one of Mercy's sons who married. He married Mary Winslow, granddaughter of General John Winslow. They had nine children in all, Mercy's only grandchildren. Henry operated the Eel River farm and helped care for his elderly parents.

John Adams did not relent in his anger at Mercy until 1813 when one of her grandchildren died. Adams was a loving grandfather, and he knew the agony the death must have caused Mercy. His condolence letter to her mended the breach between them.

In August 1814, Mercy learned that a Samuel Barrett was receiving credit as the author of *The Group*, one of Mercy's plays which had been published in pamphlet form. She wrote John Adams to ask if he remembered taking the work to the press for her to be printed.

Indeed, John Adams did remember, and he felt strongly enough about the matter to go into Boston to the Atheneum Library there and request that he be allowed to see the pamphlet.

When the librarian brought it to him, Adams saw that Mercy was correct, as a note had been written on it attributing the work to Samuel Barrett. This was an injustice to Mercy, and John Adams wrote on the pamphlet:

> August 17, 1814. The "Group" to my certain knowledge was written by Mrs. Mercy Warren of Plymouth. So certifies John Adams.

In another spot on the pamphlet he wrote:

> If the little Drama, *The Group*, had merit, it is too well known to be controverted that ... it attaches solely to Mrs. M. Warren of Plymouth, whose energies and abilities were exerted by the use of her pen on all occasions in promoting the principles that resulted in the Independence of America.

Mercy could rest now that her friend John Adams had once again affirmed his admiration for her work. A few weeks later, on October 19, 1814, Mercy Warren died.

She was buried beside her beloved James on Plymouth Burial Hill, in the same cemetery used by the original Pilgrims for the burial of their members.

Bibliography

Anthony, Katharine. *First Lady of the Revolution: The Life of Mercy Otis Warren*. Garden City, N.Y.: Doubleday, 1958.

Earle, Alice Morse. *Colonial Dames and Good Wives*. Boston: Houghton Mifflin, 1895.

Levin, Phyllis Lee. *Abigail Adams: A Biography*. New York: St. Martin's, 1987.

20

ELIZABETH
MAXWELL STEELE
(1733–1790)

Elizabeth Steele was a strong believer in the right of the colonists to seek self-government. When it appeared the British forces might emerge victorious in the Revolutionary War, Elizabeth made a timely financial contribution to the colonists' struggle.

She was born in 1733 in Pennsylvania, but while she was still a child her parents took her and her brother James to live in Rowan County in North Carolina.

Elizabeth married Robert Gillespie, a local tavern owner and operator in 1757, while her brother attended medical school in Scotland. He went to Pennsylvania to practice after he graduated.

Elizabeth and Robert had a happy marriage and two children born to them, Robert and Margaret. They also lived in Rowan County.

In 1760, Robert Gillespie, Sr., went to fight the Indians, under the command of Colonel Hugh Waddell. Indian raids had been numerous and deadly recently, and the local government did not try to protect citizens from the attacks. Gillespie and his companions believed some action was needed and they volunteered.

Elizabeth's husband was killed by the Indians, and she was left a widow at age 27, with two small children to rear alone. She continued to operate their tavern in Salisbury.

In 1763, Elizabeth married William Steele, who was the son of

Irish immigrants and who had also lived previously in Pennsylvania.

Elizabeth made William her partner in the tavern business, and it enjoyed great success. Taverns of that time were similar to today's motels. There were upstairs rooms which were rented for sleeping quarters, and meals were served in the tavern.

With so many customers coming and going each day, the Steeles were aware of political maneuverings in the colony of North Carolina and were interested in their outcome. In 1770 William Steele became a commissioner of the Borough of Salisbury.

The Regulators, who hoped to reform the local government, met in the Steeles' tavern and plotted their strategy, and Daniel Boone and his comrades planned their Kentucky exploring trips under Elizabeth's benevolent gaze.

The Regulators deplored the lack of attention to the defense of the white citizens against Indian attacks; the lack of schools, roads and bridges for all citizens; and the ever-increasing taxation imposed by the British Parliament. They believed the officials could reform and maintain a better government.

Their group numbered about 2000 men when they engaged in a battle with colonial Governor Tryon's militia at Alamance in North Carolina. Governor Tryon's men quashed the rebellion and the Regulators never were active again.

Elizabeth and William had a son born of their marriage, whom they named John. Unfortunately, William Steele died in 1773, leaving Elizabeth again a widow with a small child to rear in addition to the two children of her first marriage. Fortunately, the Gillespie children were now approaching adulthood.

Margaret Gillespie married Eusebius McCorkle, a Presbyterian minister, not long after her stepfather's death, and she started her own home and family.

Robert Gillespie continued to help his mother operate the tavern, and even nine-year-old John ran errands and made himself useful to his mother in other ways.

Neither Elizabeth nor her sons could miss hearing the revolutionary ideas expressed by various patrons of the tavern, and none of them could fail to be interested in these views and wonder what the future of North Carolina would be.

When the Revolutionary War started, Robert joined the state militia, where he attained the rank of captain.

Elizabeth continued to work in her tavern, as the war continued for six long years. She often knew as much about military events and plans as the soldiers involved, because of conversations she overheard.

Elizabeth had come to believe that the colonies should have their own government, and when Dr. Read, who was a physician for soldiers under the command of General Daniel Morgan, requested Elizabeth's permission to make the upstairs rooms of the tavern into a medical headquarters for the Colonial forces in the area, Elizabeth readily agreed.

British General Cornwallis and his troops had been keeping the Colonial forces on the run, and on January 1, 1781, General Cornwallis ordered Lieutenant Colonel Banastre Tarleton to "push (General Daniel) Morgan to the utmost. No time is to be lost!"

When Cornwallis and his soldiers advanced toward General Morgan and his men in the Kings Mountain area of North Carolina, Morgan's men moved off ahead of them. General Nathanael Greene had ordered this tactic in an attempt to divert the British soldiers.

General Morgan did not like to give the appearance that he and his men were retreating from the British, and when Morgan and his men reached Broad River just inside South Carolina at Cowpens, General Morgan ordered his soldiers to halt and stand their ground.

In the battle which ensued, the British were soundly defeated after General Morgan's forces surrounded the invaders.

General Greene was still in North Carolina, and was becoming disheartened by the way the British Army often seemed able to overwhelm Colonial troops at will. He had not heard about the colonists' success at Cowpens.

General Greene decided to visit Dr. Read and the wounded men at Steele's Tavern in Salisbury. He knew the morale of the soldiers was extremely low because of a lack of warm clothing, poor supplies of food and no pay. No money had been available to pay them for several months.

Gen. George Washington had been forced earlier to assign quotas of food to be supplied by various districts in New Jersey to keep his soldiers fed there. Since there was no central government in the colonies, there was no group to authorize money payments in order to continue the struggle for independence.

"Unless some extraordinary and immediate exertions are made by the states from which we draw our supplies, there is every appearance that the Army will infallibly disband in a fortnight," Washington wrote bluntly to the governors of the various colonies.

General Greene was acutely aware of these problems and it was a discouraged man whom Elizabeth encountered sitting at a table in her tavern that day in early 1781. Dr. Read had left his patients briefly, in order to join General Greene.

Elizabeth cooked a hot breakfast for both men, and General Greene ate with a good appetite, but he still appeared downcast and sat holding his head between his hands.

After Dr. Read excused himself to go back upstairs to his patients, Elizabeth closed the door to the dining area. She walked over to General Greene, and she assured him she and many other people in the colonies were loyal supporters of the movement for independence.

Then she took two bags of money, consisting mostly of gold coins, which she had concealed under her apron, and gave them to General Greene.

He was amazed and delighted. He told Elizabeth that the money could not have come at a better time, and all of it would go to buy food and other supplies for the Colonial army.

He looked up at a portrait of King George III which was hanging on the tavern wall, and which Elizabeth's brother had sent her from England several years before. General Greene rose, removed the picture from the wall and wrote on the back, "O George, Hide Thy Face and Mourn."

He rehung the portrait with the king's face to the wall before he rode back to join his soldiers.

135

Rumors must have reached British Army officers of Elizabeth's aid to General Greene, or it might have been coincidental, but a few days later British soldiers came to Salisbury and confiscated Elizabeth's food, horses and cattle. They broke out windows in the tavern, tore down her fences, and generally wrecked the place.

All this revenge was bad enough, but they took their actions while Elizabeth's daughter, Margaret, and her children were visiting Elizabeth. Several of Margaret's children had contracted smallpox and were very ill. The youngest child died a few days later.

General Morgan was forced to move his troops into Virginia after the Cowpens victory, because he knew additional British reinforcements would joint General Cornwallis. After a rout at Guilford County Courthouse, General Greene also moved his men into Virginia.

About this same time, French naval forces moved into position off the Virginia coast to aid the embattled Colonials. The French set up a blockade of the British garrison at Yorktown in Virginia and sent in soldiers to help the Colonials surround Cornwallis and his Army.

These efforts were successful, and the British forces surrendered at Yorktown on October 19, 1781. It was the beginning of the end of the Revolutionary War.

Elizabeth's son, Robert Gillespie, lost an eye in the war. A few years after his return home, he married a woman from Georgetown in South Carolina, located a few miles north of Charleston. He lived only two months longer, dying of yellow fever during an epidemic there.

John Steele married Dolly Nessfield in 1783, and they moved to Fayetteville, North Carolina, where he became a merchant. He was a delegate to the Fayetteville Convention in 1789 when North Carolina ratified the Constitution for the United States.

Elizabeth lived until November 1790, and had the satisfaction of seeing the new national government in place, and General George Washington elected to be its leader.

Elizabeth's contribution might be considered small in the overall scheme of financing the war effort, but assistance at just the right time can be the difference between success and failure. She may have played a bigger role than she ever knew in the establishment of a new independent government for the colonies.

Bibliography

Powell, William S. *North Carolina: A History*. Chapel Hill and London: University of N.C. Press, 1977.
Rogers, Lou. *Tar Heel Women*. Raleigh, N.C.: Warren, 1949.

21

MARY KATHERINE
GODDARD
(1738–1816)

Mary Katherine Goddard was one of the first women in the colonies to serve officially as a postmistress. She also owned and operated profitable printing businesses.

Mary Katherine was born in 1738 to Dr. Giles Goddard and his wife Sarah, in New London, Connecticut. Sarah Goddard was the daughter of Ludovick Updike, one of the members of the first settler family in Rhode Island, his father having left Germany in 1635 to come to America.

Sarah Updike was well educated for the time, as she had been allowed to study with her brothers under the direction of a French tutor. She was proficient in reading, writing and mathematics, as well as in French and Latin. In turn, she taught her daughter, Mary Katherine, the same subjects.

Dr. Giles Goddard was a prominent physician, and he served as Postmaster in New London until his death in 1757. He left his family a legacy of 780 pounds, a large amount of money for that day and age.

Mary Katherine had an older brother named William who was working as a printer's apprentice when their father died. After William's apprenticeship ended in 1762, his mother moved her family and household to Providence, Rhode Island, where she invested 300 pounds of her inheritance in setting up a printing business that she co-owned with William. William taught his mother the trade of printing.

Together the Goddards published the *Providence Gazette and Country Journal* for the next three years, while Mary Katherine, now a young lady of 24, learned to set type, which was then done by hand; how to operate the presses, and even how to ink the typeheads with leather balls which had been dipped in ink.

William lost interest in the publishing business by 1765 because, he claimed, the Rhode Island colonial government officials had not allotted him a fair share of official printing jobs. When the British Parliament passed the Stamp Act later the same year, William became an eager member of a group waging a campaign to have the law repealed.

While William maintained his resistance to the British Parliament's actions, Sarah and Mary Katherine had to assume full operation of the printing establishment. Sarah supervised the men who operated the presses and their helpers, while Mary Katherine set type.

For some time, both women had been collecting items from British publications to include in their newspaper, to give it a more international content. They also wrote original humorous accounts of various events in the area to keep readers' interest alive.

Sarah was a strong advocate of the right of women to engage in business enterprises and to take an interest in political matters or any other area of public interest. In 1766 she published a 204-page book of letters written by Lady Mary Wortley Montague, an English intellectual and feminist.

William Goddard had gone to live in Philadelphia, where he was publishing the *Pennsylvania Chronicle* in partnership with other men. Sarah cautioned her impulsive son repeatedly to hold both his tongue and his temper.

He had received good advice from his mother, but he refused to heed her admonitions. He waged a running battle with the *Pennsylvania Journal* publishers, competitors of his company, and he quarreled with his own partners. In 1767 he even published a treatise entitled "The Partnership," in which he aired his grievances to the public.

The next year, Sarah and Mary Katherine moved to Philadelphia to live with William, and Sarah bought out his interests in the *Chronicle*. Two years later, Sarah died in Philadelphia.

After his mother's death, William's problems mounted, and in 1771 he served a term in prison for debt.

When he was released from prison, William went to Baltimore, Maryland, to live, and Mary Katherine went with him. There they bought a printing business from Mrs. Nicholas Hasselbaugh, who had been trying unsuccessfully to continue working in the printing business she had inherited at her husband's death.

In 1773, Mary Katherine and William began publishing the *Maryland Journal*, Baltimore's first newspaper.

In the colony of Maryland, the mail, newspapers, and packages were delivered by the Royal Mail Service, a part of the British Imperial Post network. The postal operators were arrogant in their manner to the public, and the rates they charged were exorbitant. In addition, much mail never got to its destination, and letters were often opened and read by the postal authorities, in an attempt to find citizens disloyal to the King and his government.

It was not a good system, and William Goddard was convinced it could be improved. He could set up a better postal system than the one in place, and he voiced his belief to one and all. When his criticism of the postal service reached official ears, the Royal Mail Service refused to deliver his newspapers. Now William was forced to make good on his claim that he could do better.

First, he set up a courier service between his newspaper offices located in both Philadelphia and Baltimore. The newspapers were delivered by other carriers he hired, and he saw that his postal service idea was indeed workable.

In 1774, William suspended publication of the newspaper in Philadelphia, turned over the full operation of the Baltimore newspaper and printing business to Mary Katherine, and devoted his full attention to hiring riders to deliver letters, newspapers and packages to citizens and businesses from Maine to Georgia.

William had a really good idea at last. His mail deliverymen were much more reliable than those of the Royal Mail Service, and, before long, William's postal service had made serious inroads into the profits of the British–operated service.

According to one historian of the time, "there were frequent personal encounters and much bad blood displayed by the competing riders when they chanced to meet upon the road. These were, in effect, the preliminary skirmishes of the war that would soon break forth."

In May 1775, the second Continental Congress decided to organize and operate an official postal system for the colonies and stop the controversy. They took control of William's service and enlarged it, instead of taking over the Royal Mail Service.

Naturally, William assumed he would be put in control as Postmaster General to oversee and manage the system. His indignation knew no bounds when Benjamin Franklin was named to be Postmaster General instead of himself.

Franklin organized and ran an efficient system, which was working well by the time he went to France at the end of 1776. The Royal Mail Service had closed down officially on Christmas Day in 1775.

Benjamin Franklin knew William felt insulted by the way colonial authorities had treated him, and he offered William the job as Postmaster of Baltimore. William refused his offer, but when it was offered to Mary Katherine, she accepted, making her the first officially appointed woman postmaster in the colonies.

Mary Katherine was also still operating the Baltimore newspaper and printing business alone and profitably, while her brother had been pursuing his dream of becoming Postmaster General. When William began coming back to the Baltimore newspaper offices after his disappointment, Mary Katherine made it clear to him that she would rather continue to operate without his help. She was an expert compositor and typesetter, even according to William.

Benjamin Franklin had William appointed Surveyor or Traveling Inspector for the new postal service, and for a time William enjoyed being on the road and not tied down to work in one place. However, he quarreled with a supervisor, and, after only one year's absence, was back wanting to help Mary Katherine with the newspaper.

William had not received high marks as an inspector, and his job performance by his supervisor was rated as "careless and slovenly."

While William strolled around in Baltimore, perhaps looking for someone with whom he could disagree, Mary Katherine was honored to be asked by the Continental Congress in January 1777, to print the authenticated copies of the Declaration of Independence, showing all the signatures affixed.

That same year, William wrote an unflattering article, which appeared in the family newspaper, about the Baltimore Whig Club. As a result, he was almost literally run out of Baltimore by irate members of the club. During this time William certainly did little to enhance Mary Katherine's publishing efforts.

Mary Katherine added a book shop to her other business endeavors, while she continued to publish the weekly newspaper on time and in her own name.

William continued with his habit of insulting and criticizing everyone who disagreed with him. He was angry and upset with someone most of the time and enjoyed publicizing his troubles.

By 1784, Mary Katherine had lost patience with William and his multiple problems. When he told her he might setup a "non-competing press" in Baltimore, Mary Katherine told him not to bother—he could buy the one she had. For the first time in her life, she voiced her own complaints in an article in her newspaper.

William offered to pay her such a ridiculously low price for her share of the business, she filed five lawsuits against him in one day.

Since William had started the newspaper originally, he won the decision in court, and Mary Katherine never had any further contact with him during the rest of their lives.

William married Abigail Angell, an heiress, in 1786, and he sold the Baltimore paper and printing business to his wife's brother. William continued to hope he could get an important job with the post office.

Mary Katherine continued working in the unpaid job of postmistress in the Baltimore office after she left the newspaper, and was well liked by customers. During the Revolutionary War, she often added her own "hard money" to the receipts to compensate for the nearly worthless Continental currency she received from customers to pay for postage.

In 1789, when the new United States government began to run the country's business, money was appropriated by Congress to pay postmasters. With this change, men wanted to have the jobs, and Mary Katherine was ordered by President George Washington to surrender her job to a man named John White.

The citizens of Baltimore were outraged that she had been treated unfairly, and they sent a petition to Congress asking that Mary Katherine be returned to the position she had formerly held. Mary Katherine wrote to President Washington, making the same request.

President Washington ordered the Postmaster General to tell Mary Katherine why she was being replaced. The official reason given to her was that she would have to spend long hours on horseback, touring the area. The Postmaster General said he believed a man could do the job easier, although Mary Katherine had been told earlier that her post-office records were kept in better order than those of any of the male postmasters.

An appeal she made to the United States Senate was tabled, and it never received any official notice or action.

William Goddard had hoped to be named Secretary Comptroller of the postal system when the new government took control of the country, but that job went to Richard Bache, Benjamin Franklin's son-in-law.

Mary Katherine never married, and she spent her last years alone, except for a woman servant named Belinda Sterling. Upon Mary's death in 1816, Ms. Sterling received her freedom and all of Mary Katherine's property in her will.

Bibliography

Bird, Caroline. *Enterprising Women*. New York: David McKay, 1976.

Brooke, Geraldine. *Dames and Daughters of Colonial Days*. New York: Crowell, 1900.

Williams, Selma R. *Dementer's Daughters: The Women Who Founded America, 1587–1787*. New York: Atheneum, 1976.

22

REBECCA
BRYAN BOONE
(1739–1813)

Rebecca Boone was a pioneer's wife who willingly followed her husband into unsettled areas populated chiefly by wild animals and Indians. Without her ability to make a home for their family anywhere, it is doubtful that her husband, Daniel Boone, would have explored and opened the vast areas for settlement that he did in the new country of America.

Rebecca Bryan was born in Virginia in 1739 to Joseph and Alee Bryan, but when she was about six years old, she and her parents, grandparents and various other relatives moved to Rowan County in North Carolina. There Rebecca's grandfather, Morgan Bryan, established a settlement on the Yadkin River for himself, his eight children and their families.

The village was named, appropriately, Bryan's Settlement and was located near the homes of other Quaker families.

Most of the Bryan children already had families of their own and had established their own households—except for young William Bryan. His eye fell on Mary Boone, the daughter of neighbor Squire Boone, and the couple began a romance. The Boones, also Quakers, had recently moved to the area from Pennsylvania.

Rebecca Bryan was now 14 years old, very romantic in her thinking, and she was fascinated by her Uncle William's love affair with pretty Mary Boone. Rebecca became even more interested in the

Boones after she met Daniel Boone, Mary's brother, who was 18. Daniel largely ignored Rebecca at first, since she was a child in his mind.

The next year William Bryan and Mary Boone were married in a Quaker ceremony overseen by the bride's father. Daniel Boone attended his sister's wedding, although his real interest lay in hunting animals and exploring the vast wilderness around their homes.

Rebecca Bryan was now 15, and she had grown into a tall, black-haired, dark-eyed beauty. This time Daniel was smitten by her charms and went home to dream about her. She was now connected indirectly to his own family, and he felt she deserved closer attention. However, Rebecca showed little interest in him, which piqued his interest even more.

Rebecca may have only pretended indifference, for when she met Daniel a few weeks later at a cherry picking, she fell in love. It was a festive gathering, conducive to romance, with everyone dressed in their best clothes.

Daniel must have realized any wife of his would have to be able to look after herself and to stay cool under trying circumstances. To test Rebecca, Daniel drew his hunting knife and pretended to cut the fancy white cambric apron she was wearing.

When Rebecca only watched him calmly, without comment, he actually cut a large gash in the apron. He expected her to explode in anger, but she assured him she knew it was an accident. She may have suspected Daniel was trying her patience. If so, she passed the test, and Daniel proposed marriage to her later that same day.

According to local custom, an engaged man killed a deer, took it to his fiancée's home, and dressed the meat to indicate he could provide for her. Rebecca's giggling girlfriends were present, and, as Daniel cut the meat, the girls made teasing remarks about his skills as a butcher. They even commented on the bloody, dirty shirt he was wearing.

Daniel maintained a dignified silence during the ordeal but he was plotting his revenge. That evening, as some of his tormentors were serving his supper, he looked down at the dish at his place and said, "You, like my hunting shirt, have missed many a good washing!"

Rebecca's friends were aghast. For days after, the men in the area laughed about Daniel Boone making the girls "shut their traps."

A few weeks later Daniel volunteered to go with a group of North Carolina men to fight the French and Indians in the Pennsylvania area, under the command of General Braddock. He was gone for two years.

Rebecca should have guessed this would be a continuing pattern throughout Daniel's life, but she was in love, and she waited patiently for Daniel to return home.

On August 4, 1756, Rebecca married Daniel in a pioneer Quaker wedding. The bride rode her father's horse to the Meeting House for the ceremony, and afterward rode on Daniel's horse to their new home, which was a cabin built on Squire Boone's land.

After the ceremony, there was a lavish feast of wild game of various kinds, as well as veal, beef and pork. The meats were accompanied by side dishes of potatoes, greens and cornbread. Fiddlers played music while the wedding party and guests ate, and there was square dancing later.

Daniel had bought some land of his own before they married, and he went to work at once felling trees and dressing logs to build a cabin of their own.

Neighbors and friends came to help Daniel build their new house and two outbuildings. Wives and girlfriends of the men builders came to help Rebecca cook food for the large work crew.

Rebecca and Daniel were happy in their new marriage, and both stayed busy. Rebecca's responsibilities were cooking, cleaning and washing, as well as candle-making, plucking the geese, spinning and weaving of cloth for their clothes and drying of food for winter use each year.

The next year their first child, a son named James, was born, and two years later another son came along, whom they named Israel. Rebecca's chores increased considerably.

During these years, Daniel stayed close to home and farmed. He and Rebecca were active in their community and Meeting affairs. Other than an occasional hunting trip with some of the other men in the community, Daniel stayed home with his growing family.

Then word came that Indians were raiding villages and had massacred some white settlers nearby. Daniel understood the seriousness of the threat and feared for his family's safety. He and Rebecca took their two little boys and went to live for a time in the Fairfax, Virginia, area. To earn money for their support, Daniel worked hauling tobacco by wagon to market for a plantation neighbor living nearby.

Six months later, the Boones heard that the Indians had gone away from the Yadkin area and that other white settlers were beginning to return to their homes. Daniel and Rebecca decided to go back also.

They found the Indians had burned their cabin to the ground, and Daniel had to build another. This time he built on a 650-acre tract he had bought from his father.

Instead of farming after his return to Yadkin, Daniel began making hunting trips, during which he trapped fur-bearing animals and sold their pelts. He would be away from home for several days each time, but the money he received from the sale of the furs supported his family. Rebecca made a large garden also.

Susannah Boone was born shortly after they returned to Yadkin, and Jemima Boone was born in 1762. Now Rebecca had four young children to occupy her attention and time while Daniel continued his increasing number of forays into the wilderness.

In 1765 Daniel joined a group of hunters going to Georgia and Florida. He was gone for four months, but this time he brought back nothing but stories about alligators and swamps. He was very impressed by what he had seen in Florida. He explained he had used the animal skins he acquired during the trip to buy a homestead in Florida, in an area called Pensacola. He asked Rebecca how soon she could be ready to move to Florida.

Rebecca had abundant patience, but she must have had a bad day, or maybe they owed money to someone. For whatever reason, she told Daniel she had no intention of moving to Florida ever in her life. She was so emphatic, the subject never arose again during their life together.

Living on the frontier, Daniel constantly heard about the great hunting and trapping that could be done in the West, which at that time was really the back country of Virginia, North Carolina and east Tennessee. He enjoyed being in the open spaces outdoors anyway, and it did not take a hard push to get him started on another trek.

Daniel had been hoping to find a wilderness area where he could start a new village, as Rebecca's grandfather had done years before. The Catawba Indians told Daniel there was such a place beyond the Great Smoky Mountains; it was called "Kaintuck." They warned Daniel that two warring Indian tribes lived on the path going to Kaintuck, the Cherokee and the Shawnee. They told him he had better be ready to fight Indians.

With his long black hair worn in two braids down his back and dressed in the deerskin clothes he loved to wear, Daniel resembled an Indian himself. Only his blond eyebrows gave away his true heritage. He was not a tall man but he was fit and muscular, and he considered himself to be equal to the challenges of settling in Kaintuck (later Kentucky).

Rebecca did not object to this trip. She was beginning to understand that Daniel felt it was his life's work to explore and settle new territories which had heretofore been inhabited only by Indians.

A 12-year-old girl named Susanna Elison came to stay with Rebecca and the children while Daniel was gone. Susanna was the daughter of family friends, and Rebecca was appreciative of her help and company.

Rebecca's brother and four other men went with Daniel, having loaded their horses with blankets, food and ammunition. They traveled and camped for weeks while they slowly made their way through the Smoky Mountains in the year of 1769.

Delaware Indians lived in the area where Daniel had lived as a child, and he had friends among the Delawares. They had taught him many survival techniques to use in the wilderness, and these skills proved useful to him during his present venture.

Daniel and his companions walked through water, when it was possible, to avoid leaving footprints. They never did any hunting near their own campsite, to avoid having vultures reveal their pres-

ence when the birds sought food. Other such precautions were taken
to prevent being ambushed.

Back in Yadkin, Rebecca gave birth to a new son in December
1769, whom she named Daniel for her husband. Their family now
included three sons and four daughters.

Daniel was gone for two years. Four of the men who had gone
with him had returned earlier and they told Rebecca that Daniel was
safe and would be home in a few weeks.

When he finally got home, Daniel had many stories to tell, of
being captured by Indians and escaping from them, and of being
robbed by Indians, who had taken furs he carried. In fact, once again,
he brought home little but entertaining tales of his adventures. He
loved the Kentucky area and told Rebecca he wanted to move the
family there to make their home.

Rebecca was pregnant, and after another son named Nathan
was born in 1773, Daniel and Rebecca began making preparations
to move to Kentucky.

Daniel and other men who wanted the freedom of new horizons began building a road from Yadkin to Kentucky by way of the
Cumberland Gap, which would open up the area for any settlers or
traders who wished to travel that way. Daniel sold the land he owned
in North Carolina to Aaron Van Cleve. He and Rebecca had been
living in the Yadkin Valley for the past 17 years, but apparently he
had no regrets about leaving.

The Boones were accompanied by several other families as they
set out on horseback on the Wilderness Road that Daniel had helped
to build.

Each horse carried a passenger, clothing and some household
items. The horse on which Rebecca rode also carried two buffalo-
skin rugs and a satchel made of deerskin hooked on the saddle horn.
This was filled with wearing apparel. Daniel carried his gun and
wore an ammunition pouch around his neck.

A few household necessities, such as a homemade wire sifter, a
churn and some cooking kettles were loaded on a small flat wagon-
cart, which was pulled by a bull. Each family carried about the same
type of cargo on their horses.

Their move seemed ill-fated. On October 10, 1773, Indians attacked the party and killed James Boone, Rebecca and Daniel's oldest son. Daniel wanted to continue their journey, but the others in the party insisted that they all return to North Carolina.

Daniel realized he would have to pacify the Indians if his project were to succeed. He and other prospective settlers appealed to North Carolina merchants to finance their enterprise, and they managed to raise $50,000 which they used to pay the Cherokee Indians for the land. The sponsors expected to realize a profit from the sale of their own merchandise when the new area was opened.

In August 1775, Rebecca, Daniel and their seven children set out in another attempt to move to Kentucky. When they reached their goal, they named the village they established "Boonesboro." Rebecca was the first white woman to stand on the banks of the Kentucky River. They had no problems with Indians at all during the 300 miles they traveled.

Even after Kentucky began to be settled, it was not considered a state, but was named as a county of Virginia.

Boonesboro village was really a fort, enclosed by a log palisade and containing about 30 log cabins built within the fenced area. There were a few other cabins outside the gate of the fort; the Boones lived in one of these.

The Boone cabin contained a table made from a wooden slab, beds with wooden frames, containing either buffalo skins or feather mattresses, and chairs with seats made of deerskin. The kitchen contained large hollowed-out gourds, which were used as egg containers or to hold ground cornmeal, sugar or soap. The mantel above the fireplace held medicines, a jug of whiskey, quill pens and ink, a copy of the Bible and a tinder box.

Guns, powderhorns, clothes, hats, strings of peppers, all hung from deer antlers and wooden pegs fastened to the cabin walls.

Rebecca found her life was harder in Boonesboro than it had been in Yadkin. A son who was born not long after their move died in infancy.

One sunny Sunday afternoon, Jemima Boone, now 14 years old, and two of her girlfriends were kidnapped by Indians. While the girls were canoeing on the river near their homes, five Indian braves stepped silently and quickly out of the bushes growing along the water's edge and grabbed the boat before the girls could protest. They pulled the boat over to the riverbank, grabbed the three girls and carried them back to their camp in the forest.

Back in Boonesboro, no one realized there was a problem until none of the girls had returned by late afternoon. Daniel and his neighbors began an immediate search in the forest.

They found the empty canoe floating on the water, and even more alarming, there were moccasined footprints in the soft sand on the riverbank. As they feared, Indians had kidnapped the girls.

Jemima had not grown up in the Daniel Boone household without learning a few survival tactics of her own. As she and her friends were hurried along the trail through the dense forest, Jemima broke twigs and dragged her heels from time to time to leave traces of the path they were following.

Rebecca was frantic with worry. Would her beautiful Jemima suffer the same cruel fate at the hands of the Indians as her son James?

Daniel comforted Rebecca as best he could, and told her they would not stop their search until the girls were found and brought back home.

Next morning, Daniel and his neighbors set out early on the trail of the girls. Daniel said he felt sure it was the Shawnees who had taken the girls, as the Cherokees had given no one any trouble for the past several months. If it was the Shawnees, they would take the girls to their village and make slaves of them, as was their custom.

Daniel was correct in all his surmises. As he slipped up to the Indian encampment, he saw the girls tied to a tree. They appeared to be all right, even if they had been crying. Daniel and one of his companions each shot at an Indian brave and the others ran away. The girls were rescued and taken back home to their grateful families.

Late in 1777, Daniel went with some neighbor men to hunt for game, as their supply of food was dangerously low. However, they needed salt to preserve any meat they got, so they went to Licking River to make salt, which involved letting water evaporate from the salty water until only salt granules remained. They got caught in a snowstorm while they were working, and suddenly Shawnee braves with red and black paint on their faces came out of the heavy snowfall and captured all the men.

Daniel was dismayed at this turn of events, but he pretended he had been looking for the Shawnees so he could join their tribe, saying he was tired of farming. Daniel's fellow captives were so astonished to hear Daniel's friendly words to the Indians that some never trusted him again.

Daniel was already known by the Indians, who respected him and his reputation for tracking, hunting and finding Indians as well as game. The Shawnee chief Blackfish ordered Daniel to be tried by tribal customs. When Daniel proved to be equal to his tasks, Chief Blackfish adopted him as his own son. Even so, Daniel was under guard at all times and had no opportunity to escape. The Indians gave Daniel the name of "Sheltowee," which meant "Big Turtle."

A trader brought word to Rebecca that Daniel had been captured by Indians, and she was convinced they would kill him. After waiting for four months for his return home, she gathered their children and a few belongings together, and they all went back to Yadkin to be with her relatives there. Since Jemima had married only recently, she stayed behind with her husband, Flanders Calloway.

While his family was making their slow way back to North Carolina, Daniel finally managed to escape. He stole an Indian horse and rode as hard and as fast as he could to reach Boonesboro so he could warn the residents there that the Shawnees were planning to attack the village soon.

It took Daniel four days of steady riding to reach Boonesboro, 160 miles away. He got home on June 20, 1778, and was relieved to learn that Rebecca and their children had gone to North Carolina. However, he had no time just then to follow them.

The fort walls needed to be strengthened, a well must be dug inside the walls of the fort so the settlers could have water during the coming attack, and food had to be collected to feed everyone while they were under siege.

It was September 11, 1778, before the Indians attacked the village. By that time the settlers had grown tired of waiting, and they accused Daniel of lying about the plans he said he had heard the Indians make.

However, soon Daniel was proved correct. To the intense dismay of the Boonesboro residents, British soldiers accompanied the Indians. The Revolutionary War was raging in the eastern colonies, and the British soldiers reasoned that if they helped the Indians fight the colonists, the Indians would then help the British forces secure the area for the Crown.

The village was besieged for 10 long days while flaming arrows shot into and onto the roofs of the cabins, and screaming Indians penetrated the walls of the fort at every opportunity.

The settlers became exhausted from their efforts to defend their homes and the fort from the onslaught, and it is uncertain which group would have prevailed if heavy rain had not begun falling. The rain poured unabated for hours, and since the attackers could not fight in such a downpour, they left after an hour or so.

After resting for a few days, Daniel went to North Carolina to bring his family back to Boonesboro. He was now a major in the reserve armed forces for the colonies, having been found innocent on charges of treason brought against him for surrendering his men to their Indian attackers some months earlier.

Daniel found his family was delighted to see him, and they were anxious to get back home to Boonesboro. Surely Indian attacks were about over, they hoped.

Unfortunately, the attacks had not ceased entirely. A few weeks after their return, the Shawnees staged another raid on the village, during which Israel Boone, another of their sons, was killed.

Poor Rebecca! She must have despaired of a time ever coming when her family could live in peace without being threatened by Indians.

That really was the last raid, however, and Daniel and Rebecca began to prosper in Kentucky. In 1781 Daniel was considered to be one of the richest men in the territory. That same year, he was elected to a member of the Virginia Assembly.

Daniel filed claims to more than 75,000 acres of land in the Kentucky region during the years he and his family lived there, but he failed to complete all the steps necessary to secure his titles. He was too busy surveying land for other people.

Then the tide of his fortunes turned. Money loans he had made to friends were not repaid. Surveys he had made, guaranteeing the titles, were proved invalid and he had to pay large sums to make good his guarantees; and the land he had claimed as his own was now claimed by other settlers who had fulfilled the requirements for ownership.

In 1783 Daniel moved his family to the Limestone community on the Ohio River, where he operated a tavern and a warehouse for trading with river travelers.

In 1785 Daniel and Rebecca also opened a general store at Limestone where they sold necessities to newcomers who had begun pouring into the area. Since the new arrivals were only able to bring in items they could carry on horseback or that they could pull on small carts behind their horses, there were many items they needed to buy to start their new lives in Kentucky.

Rebecca operated the store because Daniel was busy with his other business interests and was away from home often as he continued making surveys of property in the region. She sold corn, knives, beads, kegs, moccasins, gunpowder, guns, wheat flour, blankets, flints, tobacco, shirts, and so on. The store was profitable and furnished the Boones with a comfortable living in Rebecca's capable hands.

Rebecca was now 50 years old and her children were old enough to fend for themselves, so she did not hesitate to assume operation of the store when Daniel asked her.

Daniel continued to be plagued by debts and his claims to land were overturned one by one until he finally owned none at all. By 1798, the Boones found themselves to be in dire financial circumstances. Daniel decided to try to find work of some sort.

The Wilderness Road had never been wide enough to allow

wagons to travel on it, and in 1798 the Kentucky and Virginia officials decided to have the road widened. Daniel tried to get the contract for the job, but his influence had waned, and it was awarded to another bidder.

In 1799, their son, Daniel Morgan Boone, decided to move to a new territory opening up across the Mississippi River in the Missouri area. Daniel's eyes lit up in the old familiar way when he heard the news, while Rebecca began packing, with a sigh, as she recognized the signs that she would soon be living in a new territory.

At this time, Missouri was part of the Louisiana Territory and was controlled by the Spanish government.

When the Boones arrived in Missouri, officials there welcomed them warmly, and gave Daniel a tract of land encompassing 840 acres. They had heard of Daniel's explorations and bravery, and they felt he would encourage other settlers to move to Missouri.

Daniel was getting old, and he did not build a house on his new land. Instead, he and Rebecca went to live with one of their sons and his wife for the next three years.

Each year while they lived in Missouri, Rebecca and Daniel boiled maple sap and made maple sugar. In 1800, they made 400 pounds.

They had sold their store when they left Kentucky, but Daniel continued doing land surveys, which brought in money for their support. In time he was able to return to Kentucky and pay off all their debts.

Daniel and Rebecca were beginning to feel encouraged about their future at last. They owned land and they had saved a small amount of money.

In 1804, France reclaimed the Louisiana Territory from Spain, and the area where the Boones lived was included. The next day, France sold all the territory, comprising many thousands of acres of land, to the United States government.

Daniel lost his land again, as he had received it from Spanish officials. He had not built a house on it nor cut the required number of trees from his acres, and his claim was eventually disqualified in 1809 by a federal commission.

Two of the Boones' sons had clear titles to the land where they lived. Later in 1804, Daniel and Rebecca went to live on property belonging to their son Nathan while Daniel waged his legal battle with the United States Congress to restore his own property to him.

The controversy dragged on for the next several years and Rebecca and Daniel raised large vegetable gardens and survived as best they could.

In the spring of 1813, Rebecca went with her daughter Jemima to the sugar camp, as they had done every year. They both worked hard for several weeks, boiling off the liquid to get maple sugar.

All the hard work overcame Rebecca, and she became seriously ill. She died a week later on March 18, 1813.

Daniel was devastated by grief. He obtained a legal title to his property a few months later when Congress confirmed his Missouri claim, but he did not care. With Rebecca gone, he felt his life had lost its focus.

He visited around with his various children, mostly with Jemima, still hunting and trapping when he could. He died on September 26, 1820, in Missouri at age 90. He was buried there, beside Rebecca.

Twenty-five years later, the officials of the Kentucky state government decided Daniel should rest in the state he had opened up for settlement. Missouri officials agreed to the removal of the bodies of both Rebecca and Daniel to Frankfort, Kentucky, which would be their final resting place.

A monument honoring Daniel's exploits marks their graves; there should be another for Rebecca, his loyal helpmeet.

Bibliography

Powell, William S. *North Carolina: a History.* Chapel Hill and London: University of N.C. Press, 1977.

Rogers, Lou. *Tar Heel Women.* Raleigh, N.C.: Warren, 1949.

23

MARIA VAN
HOES VAN BUREN
(1747–1817)

Maria Van Hoes was born in 1747 in the village of Claverack in upstate New York near Albany. Her Dutch grandfather had been one of the original settlers of the region, and most of the other residents in the area were also of Dutch ancestry.

Maria's last name was actually spelled "Van Goes," but was pronounced "Van Hoes" in Dutch, and when England took control of the New York colony, Maria's family began to use the phonetic spelling.

Maria was probably literate, as Dutch parents were more likely to give girls some education than the Puritans. Certainly Maria had great respect for education, and made every effort later to have her children taught subjects necessary for them to earn a good living.

In 1767, when she was 20, Maria married Johannes Van Alen, and in time gave birth to two sons and a daughter. Her eldest son, also named Johannes, changed his name to James Van Alen, and studied law when he became an adult.

James was the first of Maria's children to enjoy success in society. He became a judge and served one term in the United States Congress.

Maria's husband died in 1773, and in 1775 she married Abraham Van Buren, who was born in Albany in 1737. They went to live in Kinderhook.

157

Maria had not chosen wisely the second time, as Van Buren was a wastrel who could not seem to manage either property or money successfully. He had served as a soldier during the Revolutionary War.

Prices and values fluctuated wildly during this period of history also, but Van Buren wound up with only a tavern with which to support his family, even though his parents had been owners of a large tract of land plus the tavern.

The tavern was well located, however, being on the road between Albany and New York City, known as the Post Road.

Maria's son Martin, of her second marriage, said his father was "utterly devoid of the spirit of accumulation; his property, originally moderate, was gradually reduced until he could but illy afford to bestow the necessary means upon the education of his children."

Maria was fiercely determined that the five children born of her second marriage should receive as much education as they would take. Martin wanted to be a lawyer, like his half-brother James, and he worked during his boyhood carting cabbages from his parents' truck farm to sell in Kinderhook. Later, as he matured, he worked with his mother and father in his father's tavern.

Keeping a tavern was a respectable occupation in colonial days. With meals and sleeping quarters furnished to travelers, taverns were forerunners of our motels. They were a central part of life as well, with travelers bringing news from other areas when they got off the stagecoaches. Travelers needed rooms in which they could rest if they were continuing to travel further on a journey, and taverns filled that need. Some colonies even had laws forbidding settlers to have guests in their homes without approval from local authorities.

Perhaps it could even be said that democracy was born in taverns. With church membership in some colonies restricted to landowners and believers in particular doctrines, not all people were welcome in the churches.

In taverns, however, the aristocrat received no better service than did a ditch-digger. All political views were expressed freely by any person, and there was no class distinction of any kind.

Maria was an excellent cook and housekeeper, and keeping a tavern was an extension of housewifery skills.

According to historians, a tavern was next to the church in importance in the newly settled towns. They were similar to community centers for all activities not connected with religion.

Local men gathered after work also to exchange news and discuss local politics. Lawyers, doctors and government officials were found daily in taverns. Town meetings and sessions of Court were sometimes held in taverns when no large public building was available.

The Van Buren tavern may have been used at times for such purposes, particularly in the earlier days, and that may have led both of Maria's sons to choose law for their profession.

Taverns also furnished a way to keep alcohol consumption under control, as all taverns had to be licensed and were strictly regulated. No gambling was allowed on the premises.

As they reached school age, the Van Buren children attended Kinderhook Academy; their mother had to scrimp and save any money she got to pay their tuition.

When Martin finished his studies at the Academy, Maria asked her older son James to let Martin work as a clerk in his law office and study law with him. Since Maria had been instrumental in his own success, James agreed.

Maria and her family probably lived in a brick or stone house with a tile roof, which was the common form of construction in the area. Even outbuildings were built of these materials, with the result that Dutch communities had far fewer devastating fires than English-settled villages, which had homes built mostly of wood with thatched roofs.

Maria and all her family were members of the Dutch Reformed Church, and few spoke any English at that time. Her neighbors recalled how Maria would recite various Psalms from the Bible for comfort—always in Dutch. As time passed, Maria's children learned and spoke English.

Being members of the Dutch Reformed Church, the people in Kinderhook and other Dutch-settled villages were not as rigid in their religious beliefs and common customs as were the Puritans and other colonists. They brought the customs of Saint Nicholas (later to be called Santa Claus) and the Easter bunny to America.

At first, Dutch children in New York set their shoes on the outside of their homes to be filled with gifts on December 6, the birthday of Saint Nicholas. As years passed, they adopted Christmas Eve or Christmas Day as the time to receive gifts.

The Dutch also brought winter sports to the colonies. Being proficient ice skaters, they were glad to find the New York climate favorable for that activity. Soon the general population took part in some form of winter sports, including sledding and sleigh riding, the latter in horse-drawn sleighs.

The Dutch people enjoyed social clubs, which offered dancing and picnics, and they staged private plays; all of these diversions were frowned upon in the colonies further north. New Year's Day and May Day were celebrated with visits and family reunions.

When he finally received his law license, Martin Van Buren married a cousin, Hannah Hoes. He went into partnership with his brother James, and in 1812 was elected to serve in the New York State Senate. Maria was proud of Martin receiving such an honor, but she was even more proud when he was chosen to be Regent of the University of New York in 1815.

Martin and Hannah had four sons, and they visited Maria and Abraham frequently. They lived nearby, and the family remained close-knit.

Maria Van Buren died in February, 1817, after Martin had been named Attorney General of New York State. Abraham Van Buren died a few months later.

Martin had Maria's gravestone engraved with her first name shown as "Mary." He wanted her to be recognized as a true American with only a Dutch background. He did not mention Maria or his wife Hannah in his autobiography, as it was considered vulgar to mention women's names in print at the time.

Hannah Van Burn died in 1819, leaving four young sons for Martin to rear alone. Other than his children, few of Martin's close relatives lived to see him become President of the United States.

Maria's joy would have been overwhelming if she could have seen Martin inaugurated as President in 1837. She had worked many long hours to provide the basis for his accomplishments through education.

Bibliography

Kammen, Michael. *Colonial New York: a History*. New York: Charles Scribner's Sons, 1975.

Niven, John. *Martin Van Buren*. New York and Oxford: Oxford University Press, 1983.

24

CATHERINE
LITTLEFIELD GREENE
(1755–1814)

Catherine Greene was criticized by her contemporaries for staying with her soldier husband in field camps during the Revolutionary War, but he wanted Catherine with him and she went.

Catherine was born on February 17, 1755, to John and Phebe Ray Littlefield on Block Island, Rhode Island. Catherine's life as a child was serene and unhurried. She was called "Kitty" by her family and friends.

During her childhood, Kitty learned to ride a horse, and she became an accomplished equestrienne.

When her mother died in 1761, Kitty's Aunt Catherine and Uncle William Greene, Jr., took her to live with them in East Greenwich, and she went to school with Greenwich tutors.

Nathanael Greene, distantly related to William Greene, lived nearby and visited them often. He and Kitty liked each other immediately, and as time passed, Nathanael fell in love with Catherine with her dark flashing eyes and assured manner.

Another attraction for Nathanael in the William Greene home was the fact that both he and William believed a revolution was brewing that would overthrow British rule in the colonies, and they were heartily in favor.

It was no surprise to either relatives or friends when Kitty married Nathanael in her uncle's home on July 20, 1774, as she was now 18. Her groom was 32 years old.

Nathanael had been born and reared a Quaker, while Kitty was a member of the Church of England. Since Nathanael married outside his Quaker faith, he was put out of the Friends' Meeting in East Greenwich.

The newlyweds went to live in Coventry, Rhode Island, where Nathanael was a valued worker in family businesses which included sawmills, gristmills and the manufacture of ships' anchors.

Nathanael had always enjoyed reading, and was eager to get more education, unlike some of his brothers. Since he was a hard worker for the family enterprises, his father reluctantly agreed to allow him to be tutored in Latin, geometry, and classical literature by a Mr. Maxwell, a Scotsman.

With his broadened education about world affairs, Nathanael had come to believe that independence from England was the right path for the colonies to follow. He joined a volunteer militia group with other men from Rhode Island only days before his marriage to Kitty. He began studying military history and strategies with heightened interest as the threat of war increased.

When the Rhode Island Assembly met at Providence on April 22, 1775, to decide how best to deal with the recent British invasion at Boston, Nathanael was named Brigadier General of all the Rhode Island armed forces.

Kitty was not domestic by nature, and when Nathanael had to march off to war with his militia group, he left her in the care of his brother, Jacob, and Jacob's wife, Peggy. Jacob and Peggy took over full operation of Kitty's and Nathanael's household, as Kitty was now pregnant.

On June 2, 1775, Nathanael wrote Kitty:

> My dear wife, I am at this moment going to set off for camp....
> I have not so much in mind that wounds my peace, as the separation from you.... I had been happy for me if I could have lived a private life in peace and plenty....
>
> But the injury done my country ... calls me forth to defend our common rights, and repel the bold invaders of the sons of freedom.... I ... am, with truest regard, your loving husband, N. Greene.

George Washington was named Commander-in-Chief of the Continental Army by the Continental Congress, which met in Philadelphia in the middle of June 1775. Washington accepted the post with great reluctance, as he did not feel qualified for such a huge task. However, like Nathanael, Washington felt it was his duty to defend his country, and he accepted the position.

Before many days had passed, both men were too busy fighting British invaders to think about their former way of life. As the months passed, a friendship grew between Nathanael and Washington which would end only when Nathanael died.

Kitty could not wait to show Nathanael their new son, and she went to visit Nathanael in camp at Cambridge, and took the baby with her. Nathanael was suitably impressed by his son, and they named the little boy George Washington Greene.

Kitty returned home after a few days, only to receive a letter a short time later from Nathanael asking her to come back to camp to help him overcome a bout of jaundice. Kitty left the baby with Jacob and Peggy and went back to the Army encampment.

Kitty was a pretty woman with a vivacious personality, and she helped brighten camp life considerably. Martha Washington and some wives of other officers came to stay in the camp for several weeks.

Both Martha and George Washington were fond of Nathanael's girlish wife, whom they had met only recently, and they would all remain lifelong friends.

Kitty returned home to Rhode Island before Nathanael went on to New York. When she suggested joining him again, Nathanael urged her to leave the baby with Jacob and Peggy again as it would be too difficult to care for a baby in camp.

However, before Kitty could reach her husband, violent fighting began and she had to turn back. New York and Fort Washington were overwhelmed by British forces.

Kitty was pregnant again, and as British soldiers advanced into New Jersey, Kitty went to stay with Jacob and Peggy on their farm at Potowomut.

The new baby was a girl, and they named her Martha. Kitty

was very ill after the birth of this baby, and Nathanael worried about her.

He wrote Kitty in May 1777, that one of his aides could arrange living quarters for her about nine miles from his camp in Morristown, New Jersey, if she was able to join him.

Kitty was just as eager to see Nathanael as he was to see her, and about a month later she joined him in camp. The summer was long and hot, there was not enough food, and sanitation facilities were primitive.

In August that year, word came that British forces were entering the Chesapeake Bay area, and all the wives had to leave hurriedly for their homes.

On August 25, 1777, the British Army landed at Elk River. Nathanael wrote Kitty he had suffered a severe asthmatic attack from his exposure to the heavy dust which settled on men and horses alike. Some of the Continental Army soldiers became fed up with camp life and returned home.

As the weather grew colder, there was still a chronic lack of food and few blankets, shoes or heavier clothing for winter weather. It was December before soldiers under General Washington's command arrived at Valley Forge to spend the winter. They hastily built some log huts which were chinked with mud for shelter against the bitter cold.

Martha Washington joined her General at Valley Forge just after Christmas, and Kitty arrived in February 1778. Again she left the two babies with relatives in Rhode Island.

Many men died of starvation and exposure during the cruel winter at Valley Forge. Again, the wives of the officers did all they could to make camp life more bearable, but with so little food in reserve for men and horses, cavalry horses also starved to death. It proved to be difficult indeed for either soldiers or horses to fight with empty stomachs.

That spring, French army and naval forces came to aid the embattled American Revolutionary fighters, and the wives again returned to their homes.

Kitty was criticized harshly by some of the wives in camp

because she stayed away from her two babies for such a long time. However, Kitty knew she was now pregnant for the third time, and if the war did not end soon, she would not be able to join Nathanael in camp again.

Nathanael was named Quartermaster for the moving Army, and when local farmers and merchants preferred to sell food and supplies to British forces, General Washington ordered Nathanael to commandeer the much-needed supplies.

Nathanael performed some duties reluctantly, but he knew the soldiers must be fed. "I sent in yesterday nearly fifty head of cattle, but the country is much drained; the inhabitants cry out and beset me from all quarters...," he wrote General Washington on one occasion. Because of his successful, untiring efforts in procuring supplies for the troops, Nathanael was named Quartermaster General by the Continental Congress.

The war continued, and in February 1779, Kitty joined her husband and his fellow soldiers at Middlebrook in New Jersey. This time she brought all three of their children with her. Little Washington was now almost four years old, Martha, whom they called "Patty," was now two; and the newest Greene family member was named Cornelia.

The Middlebrook area afforded better living arrangements for the Greenes than any other place they had been. Here they had a brick house in which to live, and overall conditions were much better than they had been at Valley Forge.

Again the wives of the officers gave parties for their husbands. At one such event, Kitty danced with General Washington for three hours. Each was determined to outlast the other.

By the time Kitty packed to move her family back to Rhode Island, she was pregnant for the fourth time. She told Martha Washington she might still come to the next winter camp and have her baby there.

Martha was taken aback at such an ill-advised plan, and told Kitty she could not recommend such an action, as camp life was so uncertain and difficult. When the baby of the wife of another officer died in camp before Kitty left for home, she decided she could not risk giving birth under such bad conditions, and her husband's name-sake, Nathanael, was born in Rhode Island.

Three years would pass before Kitty saw her husband again, and then it would be in the South. On this trip she brought only seven-year-old George with her from Rhode Island, but she left him with friends in Philadelphia to begin his education.

At last the war was winding down. Nathanael was given several thousand acres of land along the Savannah River in recognition of his heroic efforts during the Revolutionary War. He and Kitty also became the owners of a home and estate called Mulberry Grove. However, until all the British forces had been driven from Charleston, South Carolina, they lived in a large house on Broad Street there.

Kitty gave a large evacuation ball to celebrate the end of the war after the Treaty of Paris was signed, after which she decided to return to the North and her children. She was pregnant again, and she found the southern climate oppressive.

Nathanael stayed behind to find an overseer and tenants for his Georgia acres. He worried about his family's financial future as the number of their children continued to increase. He believed the property in Georgia could insure a comfortable income for them.

The war had caused a severe loss in the value of money and many creditors would not accept the devalued currency as payment for debts. Nathanael and Kitty lost their home in Coventry, and Jacob and Peggy moved their family into it to live permanently.

Kitty found a house for them to rent for their family in Newport, Rhode Island, where Nathanael joined them for the winter of 1783-84.

Kitty and Nathanael's fifth child, a girl, was born in Newport, and they named her Louisa Catherine. Kitty was weakened by the birth and was unable to accompany Nathanael when he returned to Charleston in July 1784, to check on their property there.

Obligations that Nathanael had assumed for friends earlier had made his own financial picture bleak, and he was finally forced to sell the large plantation tract along the Savannah River to pay his debts. They still owned Mulberry Grove, however.

The first rice crop planted at Mulberry Grove was destroyed by a hurricane, so Nathanael turned his attention to the purchase of a wooded tract of several thousand acres on Cumberland Island. This land was heavily wooded, and he sold oak and pine lumber to help support his family.

By the fall of 1785, Nathanael was tired of commuting between Georgia and Rhode Island, and he began making preparations to move Kitty and their children to Mulberry Grove. Kitty had suggested the move earlier, because she felt they should all be living together now that the war had ended.

Nathanael realized his children needed to begin their education, and it would be more satisfactory to have a tutor live in their home. Kitty could use some help in caring for the children. He hired a young Yale graduate named Phineas Miller to tutor the children, and they all embarked for Savannah.

The large residence at Mulberry Grove was dilapidated from years of neglect, but at least the Greenes owned it, and it could be repaired and rejuvenated in time.

The Greenes settled in happily. They entertained extensively and lavishly, and for the first time Nathanael had an opportunity to play with his children and really get acquainted with them.

One of Nathanael's former Army comrades, General Anthony Wayne, decided to build a home for his own family near the Greenes at Dungeness on Cumberland Island. He was fond of both Nathanael and Kitty.

On a June day in 1786, Kitty and Nathanael went into Savannah to take care of some business affairs, and later visited with friends there overnight.

The next morning, they left early for home, but the oppressive heat of the day was already noticeable. They stopped to visit other friends named Gibbons, who lived on a rice plantation not far from their own home at Mulberry Grove. His host took Nathanael on a tour of his rice plantation, which lasted about three hours.

By the time Kitty and Nathanael got home, Nathanael had developed a severe headache. It grew progressively worse, and he died the next day, despite receiving medical attention from two physicians. Nathanael was 44.

George Washington was profoundly shocked when he heard of Nathanael's unexpected death. He wrote to a friend of Kitty's:

> I hope there will be a handsome competency for Mrs. Greene and the children, but should it turn out differently, and should Mrs. Greene, yourself, and Mr. Rutledge think (it) proper to entrust my namesake, George Washington Greene, to my care, I will give him as good an education as this country ... will afford....

Kitty was now a widow, only 30 years old, with five small children to rear alone—her last child had been born that same year.

The tutor, Phineas Miller, assumed care and control of Mulberry Grove, running all the plantation business until Kitty could hire a manager.

As time passed, Kitty decided to go back to New York and Rhode Island for a visit. She took all her children and Miller with her. All of them found the change of scenery enjoyable. In 1789, they went to New York again, which was now the temporary capital city of the new nation known as the United States of America. President Washington and First Lady Martha Washington welcomed them warmly. They dined with the Washingtons and later attended the theater with them.

President Washington came to visit Kitty and her family in May 1791, at Mulberry Grove. By now, Mr. Miller was an accepted equal and indispensable member of the Greene household, and he continued to manage plantation affairs. As a member of a well-regarded Connecticut family and with his prior education at Yale College, Mr. Miller was acceptable in all levels of society.

When another Yale graduate, who had been recommended by a mutual friend, asked Miller if he knew of a job he might get as a tutor in a Southern household, Miller told him he did.

Eli Whitney was the name of the job-seeker, and Miller told him about a family in South Carolina who wanted a tutor for their children.

Whitney came to Savannah in autumn 1792, but he was late in applying for the position, and another applicant had been chosen.

Whitney was stranded, and warm-hearted Kitty insisted that he come to live at Mulberry Grove for a time until he could find a job.

Whitney was enchanted by the lovely, gracious Kitty, whose charm had previously brightened the lives of soldiers at Valley Forge; and he was impressed by the lavish lifestyle and the exotic foods which were served at Mulberry Grove, such as rice, seafood of various kinds, watermelons and sweet potatoes.

Kitty and Miller were impressed by Whitney's willingness to make needed repairs on the estate, and by his ingenious inventions, such as toys for the children and an embroidery frame for Kitty. They urged him to stay on at Mulberry Grove indefinitely and study law, which he said was a dream of his for the future.

Most of the plantation owners in the region who raised cotton grew greenseed cotton, as it was the most successful variety for the climate of the region.

One major drawback to greenseed cotton, however, was the seeds, which were extremely difficult to remove from the cotton bolls after they were picked. It took a day for two women to clean a pound of cotton; for this reason, it was not yet profitable.

Whitney turned his inventive mind to the problem in an attempt to help Kitty and her neighbors develop an alternative source of income. Within a few days he had made a simple tabletop cotton gin, which had an internal turning cylinder, covered with small teethlike projections, to pull the cotton fibers away from the seeds. The extracted seeds then fell into a box below.

However, the fibers tended to snag and tangle on the teeth of the cylinder, and it required close attention to keep it running and frequent stops to unclog it.

When Kitty saw the gin operating, she suggested using an attached brush moving against the teeth to clean them. Her idea worked. A practical cotton gin was developed which would be of immense benefit to cotton farmers all through the southern states.

Whitney and Miller realized they had a successful marketable machine, and they formed a partnership to manufacture the gins. Whitney returned to his New Haven home to open a manufacturing plant, while Miller fought in the courts to obtain an exclusive patent for the apparatus: Imitation gins were already being built by competitors.

When the New Haven factory was destroyed in a major fire, Whitney decided not to rebuild the same type of business, but chose instead to turn to the manufacture of gun parts.

Meanwhile, Miller had been investing heavily in raw cotton in Georgia, which he could put through the gin and sell at a good profit.

Young George Washington Greene went to France to be educated at the Marquis de LaFayette's expense and insistence. Returning home after the outbreak of the French Revolution, Washington Greene drowned in 1794 when a canoe in which he was riding overturned.

In 1796, Kitty married Phineas Miller, and gave him full access to estate funds to continue in his quest for a patent for Whitney's model of a cotton gin. Without this financial aid, it is doubtful the cotton gin would have enjoyed such success.

In 1799, Kitty and Miller sold Mulberry Grove at auction and moved to the Dungeness property on Cumberland Island. The house there was a large 30-room mansion, built of a mixture of concrete, lime and seashells, mixed with water.

From this new residence, Kitty wrote to Eli Whitney in Connecticut: "We are as gay as larks and really pass our time delightfully. Company enough you know we always have. We have a party of eighteen to eat turtle with us tomorrow. I wish you were the nineteenth!"

In 1803, Miller died at age 40, and Kitty was once again a widow. All her children were grown, and her youngest daughter, Louisa, moved into the mansion to care for her mother.

Louisa was very protective of Kitty's interests and property. She may have feared Kitty might marry Eli Whitney as Whitney had never married; or perhaps Louisa hoped to marry him herself. For whatever reason, she wrote Whitney that her mother might sue him for money he owed the partnership he and Miller had formed earlier. Kitty had not even thought of such an action. She had great affection for Whitney.

Louisa also caused Kitty's estrangement from her other children, and Louisa inherited the Dungeness property at Kitty's death of yellow fever on September 2, 1814. Louisa was now Mrs. James Shaw.

Three-fourths of all the cotton produced in the United States was now grown in South Carolina and Georgia, and the market for the product steadily increased.

When Kitty died at age 59, she had not seen her good friend Eli Whitney for at least seven years, and she never knew why he did not come to see her. Whitney died in 1825.

Bibliography

James, Edward T., Ed. *Notable American Women, 1607–1950*. Cambridge: Belknap Press of Harvard University Press, 1971.

Weir, Robert M. *Colonial South Carolina: A History*. Millwood, N.Y.: KTO, 1983.

25

SARAH TODD ASTOR
(1762–1842)

The Astor family may be counted among the society Four Hundred in New York City, but the matriarch of the family had a humble beginning.

Sarah Todd was born in New York City in 1762. She was the daughter of Adam and Sarah Cox Todd, of Scottish ancestry. The little girl's father died when she was only eight years old, leaving no estate. As a result, Sarah received little if any formal education, but she was highly intelligent and interested in the world around her.

Mrs. Todd had to furnish the financial support for herself and her daughter, so she opened a boarding house at 81 Queen Street in the city. (The name was changed to Pearl Street after the Revolutionary War.) Young Sarah helped her mother by cleaning, helping prepare meals, and so on.

Sarah was washing the front doorstep one morning when a young man approached her. He was selling cakes and looking for customers. She smiled at him, and they began a conversation.

He told Sarah his name was John Jacob Astor, and that he had been born and reared in Germany. In 1780 he left Germany to go to London to stay with his older brother who was named George.

George Astor made musical instruments, flutes and other woodwinds, and John Jacob worked for him for the next three years. John Jacob told Sarah if he had not left Germany when he did, he would have had to work in his father's butcher shop. He said he would rather do almost any other work known than butchering.

Sarah was sympathetic and sensed the young man's loneliness, and she encouraged his interest in her. He told her he knew no one in New York except his employer, the baker, and another older brother, Henry Astor. When John Jacob asked Sarah if he could come back and visit, she agreed.

Sarah learned that John Jacob had had a long, hazardous ocean voyage when he left London in 1784 to come to America. The ship lacked one day of reaching Baltimore when the temperature dropped suddenly and became brutally cold, so cold that the Chesapeake Bay froze the ship fast in place.

He said many of the passengers on board left the ship and walked across the ice to Baltimore, but John Jacob stayed on board where he knew he would have food and shelter.

Other ships in the harbor were also surrounded by the ice, and passengers on other vessels visited with John Jacob and his fellow passengers while they all waited for rescue.

John Jacob encountered a fellow German from one of the ships, who was about his age and who said he had been back to Europe to find new markets for the furs he had acquired in trading with the New York Indians. He told John Jacob the profits in the sale of furs were enormous because the Indians sold them so cheaply.

John Jacob's immediate plans were to open a shop to sell musical instruments in America, so he listened with only half attention to the enthusiastic remarks made by his new friend about fur trading.

Finally, the boredom of staying cooped up on board the ship in freezing weather day after day made John Jacob decide to leave and walk across the ice as others had done earlier.

When he reached Baltimore, and found a place to stay, John Jacob wanted to see the town, so he took a walk. A little Swiss man named Nicholas Tuschdy came out of a shop he operated and began a conversation with the young German.

When Tuschdy learned John Jacob had brought a supply of musical instruments from London to sell, Tuschdy offered to put the instruments in his own shop and sell them without charging a commission, to aid a fellow European getting started in America.

In three weeks, the flutes and other instruments had sold, and John Jacob had money with which to go on to New York, where his brother Henry lived.

Henry was a butcher as their father had been, and John Jacob had no intention of asking him for a job, but he thought his brother could provide him with shelter in his home.

Henry was married to the former Dorothy Pessenger, and they were keeping house, but they had barely enough room for themselves in their small rooms. John Jacob then found lodging with a baker named George Dietrich, also from Germany, who employed John Jacob to sell his bakery products door-to-door to housewives in the area. John Jacob was selling Dietrich's cakes when he met Sarah.

Sarah's mother was impressed by John Jacob's ambition and his evident willingness to work, so she encouraged their friendship. In his spare time, John Jacob played the piano in their boarding house and entertained the Todds and their boarders by singing German songs. As weeks passed, John Jacob lost his heart completely to Sarah.

John Jacob told a grandson in later years that he had married Sarah "because she was so pretty." According to family reports, Sarah was slender, with a thin face and expressively beautiful eyes. She also possessed a large store of common sense, and she was as ambitious in her own way as John Jacob.

On September 19, 1785, Sarah married John Jacob in the German Reformed Church in New York City. Sarah brought a dowry of $300 to their marriage, and her mother allowed them to live rent-free in two rooms of her boarding house.

By the time of their marriage, John Jacob had been employed by Robert Browne, a New York furrier, for about a year. Six months earlier he had attended a trading session at a post in Albany at the behest of his employer.

John Jacob's job with the furrier was as a pelt beater. Beating the furs kept them free of moths.

In Albany John Jacob saw firsthand how trading was conducted with Indians and he was amazed at how cheaply they traded their furs. He remembered his German acquaintance on the icebound ship telling of the immense profits to be made in the fur industry, and John Jacob decided trading furs was the job he wanted. He knew he must first learn how to distinguish good pelts from poor ones, which furs were most in demand, and how to clean and care for the pelts.

Sarah urged her new husband to order more musical instruments from his brother in London, since his first supply had sold so well. He agreed when she told him to use her dowry money to pay for the instruments.

When the instruments arrived, she made a music shop in one of their two rooms in her mother's boarding house. From this location, she sold pianofortes, guitars, fifes, flutes, fine violins, and clarinets, as well as strings for the violins and guitars. She also sold music books and other necessities for musicians.

John Jacob was away from home for weeks at a time in his fur-trading ventures, and most of the time he sold his furs at auction in Albany. Occasionally, he brought some furs for Sarah to sell in the music shop.

In 1788, Sarah gave birth to a daughter whom they named Magdalen. Their second child was stillborn. When Sarah became pregnant for a third time in 1791, she urged John Jacob to buy a house so they would have room for their growing family and her music shop.

At her urging, he bought a store building, for $850, which had living quarters upstairs. Sarah was still keeping the store despite her new responsibilities, and the new location provided her with a feeling of spaciousness she liked.

By 1802, the Astors had had eight children, three of whom had died in infancy. They were both proud of their family, and were both caused profound distress when their oldest son, John Jacob, Jr., was discovered to have mental problems. They hired attendants to care for him in their home during his childhood.

President George Washington caused John Jacob some anxious moments about his lucrative fur trade when the president proposed to Congress that the United States government trade directly with the Indians and sell furs for only one-third more than the cost of doing business.

John Jacob soon realized his alarm was premature, for the government did not succeed in its venture into the fur trade. After five years, only two government trading posts had been built, and the Indians did not like trading with government officials because they did not keep liquor at their trading posts, and that was a benefit the Indians enjoyed with other traders.

John Jacob was away from home so much that his children barely knew him. He made annual fur-trading trips to Montreal and sometimes went to Europe. When he was getting furs ready for shipment, he often worked 16-hour days.

In 1802, John Jacob sold the music shop to the Piaff Brothers, and Sarah turned her talents to grading furs for her husband. Sarah told John Jacob she thought he should pay her for the fur grading she was doing as she was proficient and a better judge of furs than he. Since he had sold her music shop, she had no income of her own.

John Jacob agreed her services were extremely valuable to him, and he promised to pay her a salary of $500 an hour for the work she did for him. He paid her regularly and promptly, and Sarah used the money she earned to finance her church activities and other benevolent causes in which she was interested.

John Jacob had never really enjoyed the fur trading and his long days away from home, nor the association with rough, often unscrupulous men around the trading posts. He decided to invest in real estate in and around New York City, which he could rent for added income.

He bought a large house for his family home at 223 Broadway, formerly the home of Rufus King, the first United States Senator from New York State. He also bought a house in the country at Hellgate, which had the added attraction of being near distinguished and wealthy New York families, who would be their neighbors.

Sarah was thrilled by these developments. She felt their daughters, Magdalen, Dorothea and Eliza, as well as their younger son, William Backhouse, deserved only the best and at Hellgate the whole Astor family could get to know the "best" people. Their disabled son had not improved in any way.

For years Sarah had insisted that the whole family attend a

church whose membership included bankers and lawyers, and she encouraged John Jacob to join the Masonic Lodge.

John Jacob, despite his wealth, was something of a diamond in the rough, and he really preferred working to socializing, but Sarah was determined. They soon numbered United States Senator Aaron Burr, General Stephen Van Rensselaer of Albany, and other notables among their friends and acquaintances.

John Jacob's real estate transactions were only a hobby with him now as he had turned his attention to trading in the Orient, and his real interest was the trade with China. He shipped furs from seals, foxes, otters and beavers, which he obtained for almost nothing, as well as large quantities of ginseng, a wild plant harvested for its roots and prized in China as an aphrodisiac. When his ships returned, they brought back China silks, delicate shawls and fans of the finest workmanship, Chinaware and thousands of pounds of China tea. All these products sold well and at a high profit in the United States.

When the Astor children began marrying, John Jacob took an active interest in their choice of partners. When Magdalen divorced her first husband, Governor Adrien Bentzon of the Danish West Indies, whom she had married in 1807, her father supported her in her decision, even though the divorce created a scandal in New York society in 1819.

Sarah also felt Magdalen was justified, as her husband admitted he had committed adultery, but other Astor relatives said Magdalen was spoiled by her wealth and influence and was arrogant.

Magdalen married John Bristed from England later that year, and they had a son whom they named Charles. Charles became his grandfather's favorite.

Dorothea Astor married Col. Walter Langdon about 1813, after a whirlwind courtship. Col. Langdon had no wealth and worked as a staff member for the governor of New Hampshire.

William Backhouse Astor, born in 1792, was trained from an early age to take over his father's business interests. William attended a private school in Connecticut until he was 16, then spent the next eight years studying at Heidelberg University and Göttingen University in Europe.

William was scholarly and enjoyed studying and traveling; however, his father insisted that he return home in 1816.

In 1818, William married Margaret Armstrong, daughter of Gen. John Armstrong, who had been a friend of the Astors for many years. John Jacob was pleased with William's selection of a wife and made him a partner immediately in John J. Astor and Sons enterprises.

John Jacob was not happy with Dorothea's choice of a husband, however, feeling she had not used good judgment in selecting a man with no money, and he would not even visit her.

In 1818, John Jacob saw a pretty little girl at a children's party who reminded him of his wife Sarah, and he asked the child what her name was. She told him she was Sarah Langdon, Dorothea's daughter. John Jacob then admitted he was her grandfather, and he went to visit his daughter, and the family was reconciled.

Eliza, who was born in 1801, was the family pet. She resembled her mother Sarah in her piety and participation in religious activities. When John Jacob decided a trip to Paris might effect a cure for his disabled son in 1820, Eliza went with them, as did a nurse. Sarah's health was not good and she did not want to go.

While in Europe, Eliza met and married Count Vincent Rumpff of Switzerland, who was Acting Minister to France for his country's government.

John Jacob bought a villa on Lake Geneva in 1824 for $50,000, and he and Eliza spent happy hours there, attending concerts, the theatre, and other events. Sadly, Eliza died in 1832.

John Jacob's beloved Sarah also died while he was in Europe in 1832, as well as their daughter Magdalen.

All of these deaths of his nearest and dearest relatives had a negative effect on John Jacob's health, and in the latter part of 1832 he returned to Europe to consult doctors there about his nerves.

He received treatment for about 18 months, and even celebrated his 70th birthday in Paris. On his return voyage to New York, the ship encountered a severe storm at sea, and John Jacob's nervous problems recurred.

Back home, John Jacob tried to find relief from depression in working harder than ever. He sold his fur company in 1834, and started having a luxury hotel built in New York City that year. It was called the Astor House, and was by far the most elaborate such establishment built in the United States up to that time.

Astor House was 6 stories high and contained 300 bedrooms and 17 bathrooms. Furnishings were made of elegant black walnut wood. The restaurant in the hotel served the finest food. Room rates, at $2 a day, were considered to be exorbitant.

The Astor House project kept John Jacob's mind occupied and helped him overcome his deep grief about his family losses.

Unfortunately, the trip to Europe did not improve young John Jacob's mental state, and in 1838 his father built a house in New York, especially for his disabled son, which was surrounded by a high wall. Here the young man could walk and exercise freely away from the curious eyes of the public. He lived to be 78 years old.

John Jacob, Sr., died on March 29, 1848, after a long period of declining health. His fortune, distributed among his many relatives, was estimated to be about $25,000,000.

Bibliography

Cowles, Virginia Spencer. *The Astors.* New York: Alfred A. Knopf, 1979.
Klein, Milton M., Ed. *The Empire State: A History of New York.* Ithaca and London: Cornell University Press, 2001.

INDEX

Index